THE TOURETTES SURVIVAL KIT

by the same author

Tic Disorders
A Guide for Parents and Professionals
Uttom Chowdhury and Tara Murphy
Foreword by Suzanne Dobson, Chief Executive of Tourettes Action UK
ISBN 978 1 84905 061 6
eISBN 978 0 85700 917 3

of related interest

Can I tell you about Tourette Syndrome?
A guide for friends, family and professionals
Mal Leicester
Illustrated by Apsley
ISBN 978 1 84905 407 2
eISBN 978 0 85700 806 0
Part of the Can I tell you about…? *series*

Why Do You Do That?
A Book about Tourette Syndrome for Children and Young People
Uttom Chowdhury and Mary Robertson
Illustrated by Liz Whallett
ISBN 978 1 84310 395 0
eISBN 978 1 84642 491 5

**Kids in the Syndrome Mix of ADHD, LD, Autism
Spectrum, Tourette's, Anxiety, and More!**
The one-stop guide for parents, teachers, and other professionals
Martin L. Kutscher, MD
With contributions from Tony Attwood, PhD and Robert R. Wolff, MD
ISBN 978 1 84905 967 1
eISBN 978 0 85700 882 4

The Neurodiverse Classroom
**A Teacher's Guide to Individual Learning
Needs and How to Meet Them**
Victoria Honeybourne
ISBN 978 1 78592 362 3
eISBN 978 1 78450 703 9

THE TOURETTES SURVIVAL KIT

TOOLS FOR YOUNG ADULTS WITH TICS

TARA MURPHY AND DAMON MILLAR
ILLUSTRATED BY HIRO ENOKI

Jessica Kingsley *Publishers*
London and Philadelphia

First published in 2019
by Jessica Kingsley Publishers
73 Collier Street
London N1 9BE, UK
and
400 Market Street, Suite 400
Philadelphia, PA 19106, USA

www.jkp.com

Library of Congress Cataloging in Publication Data
A CIP catalog record for this book is available from the Library of Congress

British Library Cataloguing in Publication Data
A CIP catalogue record for this book is available from the British Library

ISBN 978 1 78592 359 3
eISBN 978 1 78450 700 8

Printed and bound in the United States

INTRODUCTION

This isn't a normal book, it's a survival kit. Survival kits are useful for whatever challenge you're facing right now:

 If you're facing a challenge, choose the **situation** you're in, and go.

 If you have time, get skilled up with **tools** that will help you.

 If you need to explain tics to **other people**, flip to the back of the book.

school

jobs

home

love

driving

transport

occasions

situations

what is Tourettes?

living with Tourettes

treatments

tools

for other people

MEET THE SUPPORT CREW

Dr Tara

Welcome to this Survival Kit. I am a psychologist and have worked with people who have tics for many years. Tic disorders have many different names, Tourettes, Tourette syndrome, Tourette disorder. In this book we will call it 'Tourettes' because that's what most people who have it call it. I've heard about lots of challenges and solutions from the people I have worked with and wanted to include them in a book, so here we go!

Dr Jolande

Hi! My name is Jolande van de Griendt. I'm a health psychologist and cognitive behavioural therapist from the Netherlands. I run a telemedicine private practice in behavioural treatment for tics (called 'ticxperts') and am doing a PhD comparing medication versus a behavioural treatment called 'exposure and response prevention' (ERP). Together with Tara Murphy, I run behavioural treatment workshops for professionals all over Europe.

Duncan

Hello there. I'm Duncan McKinlay, aka 'Dr Dunc', a registered psychologist with the College of Psychologists of Ontario, Canada, practising with children and adolescents in clinical and school psychology. I was diagnosed with Tourettes at age 19 but knew that I had a 'secret' by age seven. I am a past director of the Tourette Syndrome Foundation of Canada, and have received numerous awards for my professional work, and sit on professional advisory boards for various Tourettes organisations. You can read about me, watch my documentary or purchase my book *Nix Your Tics!* by logging on to my website, 'Life's a Twitch!' (www.lifesatwitch.com).

Mike

I'm Mike. I've held leadership roles in a number of multinational and global organisations, including head legal counsel and chair. Most recently I founded a number of technology businesses. I speak to audiences of up to 5000 people and chair conferences, dinners and media events in many parts of the world. I am also an ultra-distance runner and compete at an international level. I have Tourettes.

Rupert

I was diagnosed with Tourettes when I was ten, which was four years ago. During that time I have found many ways to deal with my tics on a daily basis but no day is ever the same. It takes great concentration and willpower, and I find having a positive attitude is the key to my challenging situation.

Daniel

I'm Daniel. I'm 24 years old and have had Tourettes for most of my life. Since being diagnosed at the age of nine I've always looked for ways to ensure my tics stay a relatively small part of my life. I'm currently living and working in the Canadian Rockies as part of a year out from my career.

Liz

Hello, I'm Liz, a psychologist who delivers online behavioural therapy for tics and Tourettes to people over 18 years old.
I have adult-onset Tourettes. A couple of years ago I experienced a meditation session which helped reduce the frequency and intensity of a particular tic and led to the eventual development of 'At ease with your tics: A guided relaxation', a relaxation exercise that has been developed through the diverse skills of a meditation teacher, a musician and Tourettes

healthcare professionals. You can find it at www.tourettes-action.org.uk/news-276-guided-relaxation-for-tics.html

Eliza

Hi, I'm Eliza. I'm 15 years old and have had tics since I was four. I used to be bothered by the tics, but once I realised that the tics were not that important, I stopped caring about them so much. Now I'm the boss.

Jess

Hi, I'm Jess, co-founder of Touretteshero. Artist, performer, playworker and expert fundraiser, I've had tics since I was a child but wasn't diagnosed with Tourettes until I was in my twenties. With some encouragement from my friends, I have turned my tics into a source of imaginative creativity and the Touretteshero project was born: www.touretteshero.com

Harry

Hiya. My name is Harry and I'm 15 years old, nearly 16. I got tics at nine years old and don't mind them TOO much, but sometimes they really annoy me. I have found some good ways of managing the tics at school. I also have attention deficit hyperactivity disorder (ADHD). I'm a fictional person, made up from aspects of many young people Dr Tara has seen over the years, so my profile picture is a sketch.

Megan

Hello, my name is Megan. I'm 19 years old and find that I can outwit my tics. Sometimes they get to me but I have worked out several excellent strategies to help me. I'm a fictional person, so my profile picture is a sketch.

Zak

Hi there, I'm Zak. I'm 23 years old and I work as a personal trainer. I've had tics since I was five years old. The tics have always been a part of me and I've just learned to live with them. I think I'd miss them if they disappeared. I'm a fictional person and that's why my profile picture is a sketch.

SITUATIONS

What situation are you facing?

Whether you've got a month to prepare or it's happening right now, find your situation here, and we will give you immediate help.

Managing tics at school, college or university

Schools are full of different sorts of people, so they have methods to support different learning needs. Students with Tourettes are able to learn well.

Starting school

You

It's my first day in a new school. There's lots to worry about and I want to make a good impression. What can I do?

One month before

Megan

Contact the special educational needs teacher.
Send them helpful information on Tourettes
and tics, to make sure they know what is
happening and how to help you. Even with plenty of
brains and attitude, it helps to have someone else who
understands. Try to make an appointment to see the
teacher who deals with additional needs (see Tools →
Community).

school

Harry

*Ask your doctor for a medical note to show that
you need additional support.* I like cunning
solutions that give me the edge in solving
problems, so it's great to get extra support like
accommodations for extra time in exams, a separate
space or a scribe to write for you. In school there is
more than one way to give you extra help for tics; it
needs to be bespoke for your particular needs. If you
have additional learning difficulties, like problems with
reading, writing or maths, then you might need more
support (see Tools → Tourettes plus other difficulties).

Rupert

Do a presentation. Giving a talk or showing a
film on Tourettes helps to educate teachers
and students about the issues at an early
stage rather than waiting for misunderstandings
to occur.

school

One week before

Dr Tara

Tics can be particularly troublesome at the beginning of term, so update your school or college just before you start.

Harry

Help people understand about tics. Setting other people straight about what tics are (and are not) can be helpful from the start. Most people are understanding. Practise explaining tics to people, until you get good at it. See if you can get your explanation off-hand enough that people don't worry about tics. I had a classmate who was diabetic – he would casually whip out a syringe and inject himself mid-sentence. His nonchalance made it clear that there was nothing to worry about or even discuss. Try to give people that sort of casual explanation (see Tools → Explaining your tics to other people).

Megan

Choose where to make your first impression. Some situations combine with tics to make it difficult to make a good first impression (e.g. introducing yourself to the class might make you tic). Figure out what those difficult situations are, and plan ways to avoid them so you make a good first

impression in places you are at your best (see Tools →
Avoiding stereotypes and misunderstanding).

school

Zak

Get peer support. Contact a classmate or
another person who will be on your course. I'm
into martial arts, and like to think I can handle
situations myself, but I still find it really helpful to have
an ally who can speak up for me if I'm struggling
(see Tools → Community).

Liz

Prepare for pressure. In training sessions at
work or listening to long lectures where you
have to sit for hours at a time (longer than you
can usually go without ticcing), prepare beforehand.
Tell whoever is organising the event that you might
need some private tic time.

Megan

Find strategies for your hard tics. You probably
already know which of your tics will give you
trouble in school. Eye tics can make reading
tricky and motor tics can get in the way of writing
easily, but there are ways around most tics (see
Tools → School).

Tomorrow

 school

Zak

Get your mind calm. Remind yourself of how well you have handled similar situations in the past (see Tools → Positive attitude).

Dr Tara

Positive self-talk. Make sure you are saying positive things to yourself that make you believe that you can succeed. If you catch yourself saying 'I'll never manage it', replace those words with 'This time I will make it.' Remember that the biggest predictor of whether you will succeed is that you think you will.

Megan

Review and be ready. Review the useful strategies you have worked on and decide which of them you will use tomorrow.

Harry

Positive story. To strangers, we are who we say we are. Find a story that makes you who you are – and who you want to be. Practise it.

Today

Zak
Give yourself time and space. Wake up early and give yourself time to get ready.

Harry
Use strategies to help you to stay calm. If you can, travel to school with a friend who knows you well and can distract you from worrying thoughts (see Tools → Treatments).

Dr Tara
Get anxiety under control. You may not be able to stop all tics, but you can help reduce anxiety. Listen to your body to know if you are anxious, such as having fast breathing and tense shoulders. If a problem emerges then use problem-solving techniques to break down the dilemma and fix it (see Tools → Problem solving).

Megan
Check in before lessons. See the teacher you have been liaising with about support and check in with them before class starts, if you can. Teachers are busy the first day too.

Jess

Explain about tics, many will appreciate it. I once got into trouble with a teacher for throwing a basketball at him when he'd just told us to put them down. I was shocked by how I'd behaved and worried about his response. He didn't know I had Tourettes (and neither did I then), but I explained that I hadn't chosen to throw the ball and he listened to me. Some adults will listen and understand; others may need more help learning about the best ways to support you.

In the classroom

You

I keep disturbing the class, and when I'm not disturbing other people I'm fighting with myself not to disturb other people. It makes classrooms a really hard place to learn. What can I do?

school

Tell the teacher about having Tourettes

This month

Rupert

Be flexible. The classroom is a quiet time where tics are more noticeable. I have found many ways to deal with my tics on a daily basis but no day is ever the same, so have many strategies.

Zak

Sort out any other problems you have. Most people with tics survive and learn well in school, but tics are harder to manage if you have other problems, like poor attention, severe anxiety or low mood. Many of these difficulties are more effectively changed than tics, so do yourself a favour and get them sorted (see Tools → Tourettes plus other difficulties).

Jess

Focus on what matters. I used to find written work difficult because I wanted my handwriting to be perfect; the obsessive part of my brain wanted me to start again each time I felt it wasn't perfect. This made writing very slow, but when I talked to my teacher about it, they told me it was ideas in my work that mattered, not how it looked.

Harry

Try to find your triggers. Figure out which places and situations make you tic. Learn how the triggering situations develop, so you can see the early signs of menacing tic situations forming, and put strategies into place to manage. It's best not to avoid situations as you can miss out (see Tools → Tic triggers).

school

Jess

Work out what helps you concentrate. I used to record my lessons and then I would listen back to them while I walked the dog; I found it much easier to concentrate when I was moving.

Rupert

Time out can help. Time out cards are also great to allow you to leave the class early or if you are unable to deal with the tic.

Jess

Breaks from the classroom. At school my teachers used to give me jobs to do outside of the classroom; this helped me because it meant I could move around and make noise on a regular basis – you could try asking your teacher for movement breaks from class.

school

Tomorrow

Dr Tara

Choose a good place to sit. Scope out a place in class where your tics won't annoy other people. Maybe choose a place at the side, so that your classmates won't see the tics as easily. Make sure you are close enough to the teacher – the more engaged you are with the lesson, the less you'll be worried about other people's reaction.

Megan

Contact your teacher. Speak with or email your teacher if your tics are particularly noticeable and explain what you are doing to manage and what they can do to help you (see Tools → Teachers/lecturers).

Rupert

Get in there early. Waiting until the end of the class to talk to the teacher is too late as the stress and anguish would already have occurred.

Daniel

Make sure they get it. If you ask your teacher to say something to the class, make sure they understand tics fully first. The most

well-intentioned teacher can still accidently
spread misinformation.

Today

school

Zak

*Focus your energy until the urge to tic reduces or
is weak.* Find a competing activity that helps
you to not tic, or to tolerate the urge and not
let the tic out (see Tools → Behavioural therapy).

Megan

*Try to find something you can do without anyone
noticing.* Perfectly drum with your foot the
beat to your favourite music track to distract
from your tics.

Mike

Sneak a few tics out. I found that resisting
and managing tics in the classroom can be
really tiring. I found it useful to cover my face
with my hands as if yawning or rubbing my eyes or
forehead, as a way to sneak some tics in for a bit of
relief. Actually focusing on what the teacher or others
are saying also helps. This trick works later in life too.

Harry

Disguise tics. Your tics may be small or quiet enough that you can disguise them. Disguising a tic can be less stressful than controlling them (see Tools → Disguise).

Eliza

Choose your tic timing. I try to do the tics when people aren't looking. If you are doing a presentation, really concentrate on not ticcing then. It helps to tell the teacher.

Megan

Leave class and get the notes. If your tics are out of control, then neither you nor anyone else is going to learn much.

Dr Tara

Laugh a little. Being serious all the time can be draining. Laughter puts us all on the same side – we laugh together. Only you can make it okay to laugh at your tics.

Jess

Talk to your teachers. I used to try and save my tics up and let them out in the toilet at school; I didn't tell anybody what I was doing. This was very tiring and it meant I couldn't concentrate on my lessons and I worried about what other people thought. I would've been much happier if I'd talked to my teachers and friends and not tried to change myself.

 Library/assembly

You

I hate quiet, still places, because groups of quiet, bored people make a big audience for my tics. What can I do?

One month before

Megan

Ask to be excused in exceptional circumstances. If your tics are often big, ask your teacher in advance whether it will be okay to be excused until the tic reduces or is manageable.

Zak

Practise competing responses. Using a competing response can help you to substitute a less noticable sound or movement for the tic (see Tools → Habit reversal training).

school

This week

Daniel

Be creative about where you study. I always avoid silent places. For example, throughout university I studied in cafes rather than libraries. It's just not worth the stress.

Tomorrow

Megan

Plan a space for ticcing before and after the event. Look for places you can use tomorrow, where you will be able to tic without anyone noticing or being distracted.

Today

Harry

Move to a low-profile place in the group. Find a position in the group where nobody will notice you ticcing. The best place is usually the side of the class.

Dr Tara

Stop reading. If you're reading this book during assembly, you probably shouldn't be!

Exams

Tics needn't really be a big problem in exams, so long as you find a way to accommodate them.

You

I need to focus on my exams. Everyone else needs to focus too! That's not easy when I'm ticcing. What can I do?

One month before

Dr Tara

Get a formal diagnosis. All schools need you to have a formal diagnosis of Tourettes before they can give you exam accommodations. Specialists often have a waiting list that's months long, so organise an assessment early (see Tools → What is Tourettes?).

Megan

Ask for extra help. There are some types of assistance you can get to help you cope with Tourettes in exams, like extra time and exercise breaks (see Tools → School).

Daniel

Separate space. Some schools may be able to give you a separate room for exams or help you in other ways. Make sure you discuss your options with your school well in advance so you can focus on your studies when the time comes.

One week before

Zak

Ramp up the sleep. Start planning sleep so you have several early nights 'in the bank'. Tics are worse when you are tired, and nobody sleeps well during exams (see Tools → Treatments).

Megan

Study. The more you know the less anxious you will be.

Dr Tara

Make a plan for tic attacks. Tic attacks often occur when people are nervous about something. Ensure that there is a plan of how to cope if you have a tic attack. It's good to plan with other people NOT to call an ambulance for help as we know that this is not usually needed (see Tools → Tic attacks).

Tomorrow

Harry
Find a space for ticcing before and after the exam. Find places where you will be able to tic without anyone being distracted. Make sure that the places are close enough to reach quickly.

Today

Zak
Meditate. It may sound crazy, but 10 minutes of calm mindfulness before the exam is much more useful than another 10 minutes of panicked study (unless you've only done 10 minutes' study!) (see Tools → Treatments).

Megan
Move. If you're annoying other people.

 Bullying

Bullies will use anything unusual about you to comment on, so tics are an obvious target. Remember that bullies are just looking for a button and a person who responds when it is pressed.

school

> **You**
> I'm getting bullied about my tics. What can I do?

Confront people who tease you by explaining it's not something you can help

This month

> **Dr Tara**
> *Get official help.* Find out who the official person is who deals with bullying or harassment at school/college/university, and make sure that they know what is going on. You can have powerful allies against the bullies just by asking for help (see Tools → School). Bullies will sometimes

try to make you feel bad for getting help, but don't let their whinging get under your skin.

Zak

Learn a martial art. Bullying is a power difference. Remove that power difference by becoming more powerful (see Tools → Exercise).

Megan

Look for groups who accept and celebrate diversity. Bullying only exists where it is accepted or tolerated. I usually come across bullying in places where there is pressure to conform to a single 'norm' or ideal. But some groups or places encourage multiple roles and that's a lot more fun! Just like in the circus, not everyone can be the juggler; you also need a trapeze artist and a clown. A circus with just jugglers would be boring!

This week

Dr Tara

Learn to ignore insults. Bullies are looking for a reaction, so don't give them one. Like circling buzzards, bullies are attracted to people alone, so ask a friend to join you when bullies give you trouble.

Tomorrow

Harry

Plan a space for ticcing away from bullies.
If ticcing triggers bullying, then make sure
you do your ticcing where bullies can't see it.

Daniel

Keep strong. Kids will find any excuse to bully
someone. The problem is always with the
bully, not you, and will go away as soon as
your classmates grow up.

Today

Harry

Change your reaction. Bullies only persist
because they get something they want from
the interaction. Figure out what that thing
they want is, and deny them it. If they want to see you
lose your temper, stay calm. If they want to humiliate
you, stay proud. The first time you deny a bully what
they want, they will push harder to get the response
they used to like; they will eventually get bored and
find some other entertainment.

Eliza

Give them 'the look'. When I was younger
I would have just cried when bullied but

now I'm older I know I would just give them a look. Everyone has something different about them, so it is not a big deal.

school

Zak

Fake confidence. If you have been bullied before, it's easy to be anxious about it happening again. Bullies look for anxious people. Identify confident people and copy what they do. 'Fake it to make it' means that although confidence starts off fake, it'll become real over time! (See Tools → Self-esteem.)

Mike

Give people the benefit of the doubt. It is important not to confuse surprise or interest with bullying or prejudice. What I mean by this is, if someone suddenly sees a tic and it is the first time they have seen you do it, then they will not have been expecting it and they may look surprised or puzzled for a moment. You may see this in their face. That does not mean that they have formed a negative view, or care that you have done it; they just weren't expecting it.

Megan

Don't take it to heart. Some things bullies say can keep going around in your head. Don't let them. Imagine they are saying 'blah blah blah' when they open their mouths. Don't fill your head with their nonsense.

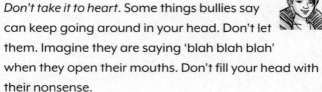

Jess

Set boundaries on others' responses to tics. It can be hard to know what to do when people make fun of your tics and pretend it's just a joke. I explain that I'm happy to talk about them and answer questions, but it hurts my feelings if people copy them or laugh behind my back.

Liz

Bullying comes in all forms. What if bullying or discrimination comes from someone in charge who should be providing help, a person in a position of trust, power or authority? This is very important to deal with. If you feel that a senior person is bullying then discuss your concerns with a trusted adult, or a supportive organisation such as a local Tourettes charity or your Citizens Advice Bureau that can offer advice.

Getting and working a job

Getting a job is an important part of growing up. It provides independence, gives you money and broadens the group of people you will see regularly. This new situation may also provide new challenges for coping with tics.

 ## Curriculum Vitae (CV)/resume

You
I'm writing a CV and I don't know whether to mention my tics, and what to say about them. What should I write?

One month before

Megan
Be who you want to be. When you're writing a CV, it's time to think about who you are and who you want to be.

Dr Tara
Think about whether to mention Tourettes. This is a personal choice. Should you put Tourettes on your CV so you don't shock the interviewer and stress yourself? Or should you leave it off because it's hard enough to get an interview anyway, without an employer being confused about what tics are?

35

If you choose to mention Tourettes in your CV, make sure it's at the end, so they see who you are first. Be clear about the severity and how much the tics will impact on your ability to do the job.

Jess

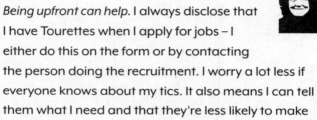

Being upfront can help. I always disclose that I have Tourettes when I apply for jobs – I either do this on the form or by contacting the person doing the recruitment. I worry a lot less if everyone knows about my tics. It also means I can tell them what I need and that they're less likely to make assumptions.

Liz

Who needs to know? If you don't actually tic at work for most of the time, ask Occupational Health for support and to help you figure out how much confidentiality you need to feel comfortable.

Megan

Talk to the careers advisor. Get some advice on what job or role looks good for your experience.

Harry

Find out the 'must have' points for the job you want. You won't get the job unless you have these 'essential' things. Can you get experience in that area? Just enough to tick the box?

One week before

Zak

Set up an internet presence. Consider getting a LinkedIn profile and setting up an email address with a professional name, not a personal one (i.e. not 'bigpantszaccy@hotmail.com').

Tomorrow

Dr Tara

Find a style and CV template you like. Choose a style that fits the format that people in your industry expect, but customise it so it says who you are. Ask to look at an example CV from someone you know, to get inspiration. Make sure it's someone who has been successful in getting a job or two!

Today

Megan
Summarise yourself. Put a one-sentence summary of who you are at the top of the first page. It helps people remember you and shows your strengths at the start.

Zak
Keep it brief, but complete. Keep the CV short – I like to stick to one to two pages. Make sure it gives a good sense of who you are and what you have to offer.

Choosing a job

Whether it's a part-time job or the start of a lifelong career, selecting your job is really important. You'll be spending many hours in the job, so it's worth the work at the start.

You
I'm wondering about what kind of job I can do and if my tics might get in the way. It's more difficult than school because I need to do it all myself.

One month before

Dr Tara

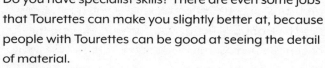

Know your abilities. Try to understand the 'shape' of your abilities and qualifications. Are you skilled with people? An analytical thinker? Do you have specialist skills? There are even some jobs that Tourettes can make you slightly better at, because people with Tourettes can be good at seeing the detail of material.

Mike

Controlling your tics can make you mentally strong. As someone with Tourettes I am used to being a bit uncomfortable most of the time. And I am practised at ignoring and resisting the uncomfortable feelings in order to resist ticcing. As a long distance runner, the ability to ignore discomfort is essential for success. Tourettes has given me additional levels of mental strength to cope with pain and discomfort when I am racing long distances.

Duncan

Find your niche. A disorder doesn't have to be a disorder if you find an environment that matches it. I found mine – I'm a psychologist and work with children and adolescents in the areas of clinical and school psychology.

jobs

Zak

Find the limits of jobs. Most jobs are just fine with tics, but there are some jobs you probably should think carefully about and some jobs you should avoid. The jobs to be careful of are ones where tics cause 'Health and Safety problems' or could 'offend clients'. If you have strong tics, think about whether you can work around the tics or control them. Some medications for tics may advise you against operating heavy machinery (see Tools → Medication).

Mike

Do whatever you want to do. There are very few jobs that Tourettes gets in the way of doing; making a living as one of those 'human statues' would be a big ask, but apart from that, most things would be a go!

Jobs

*Be clear on how your tics impact you;
don't let people make assumptions*

Dr Tara

Find your own limits. Tics are not the same everywhere. Some people find that when they concentrate very hard on a topic, their tics stop happening. There are surgeons, airline pilots, drivers, comedians, hairdressers and top sports people who tic! The trick is to learn what makes you tic, and avoid jobs where that's going to be a problem. Finding out the limit of your particular tics may take hours of practice, so try to get some practical hands-on experience before choosing a career.

jobs

Zak

Get official documentation. It can be helpful to have a letter from a health professional saying that you are capable of doing a job with your tics (see Tools → Getting a diagnosis of Tourettes).

Jess

Know your rights. It's important to know that nobody can discriminate against you for having tics at work. If you live in the UK, learning about the Equality Act 2010, which is a piece of legislation that protects people with particular conditions or characteristics from discrimination, it helped me know my rights and feel confident asking for the support I needed. The Equality Act says anyone providing a service has to make 'reasonable adjustments' for you if you need them to. This could mean providing a piece of equipment, doing something in a different way, or being flexible about their rules. If you live outside the UK, find legislation that helps you to access the support you need.

Megan

Learn what work discrimination looks like. Restrictions and discrimination are not always obvious. Even slight discrimination can eventually lead to disadvantages in skills, so it's important to discuss it with the employer or recruiter if you see it. Signs to look out for are if you meet all the job criteria but don't get an interview, or if someone asks more questions about your disability than your abilities. Be careful because not every concern is discrimination; employers may be uninformed about Tourettes, or may have reasonable concerns (e.g. how you could work in an open plan office with loud vocal tics).

jobs

Dr Tara

Find a job that fits you. Look at the job market to see what jobs you would be good at. Ask around, because many jobs are never advertised.

One week before

Zak

Look for a job. Search online, at your local job centre, or with some help from a family member or friend. Go and visit the workplaces and ask questions.

Tomorrow

Harry
Narrow down the choices. From all the jobs you have looked at, find the best (see Tools → Problem solving).

Today

Dr Tara
Make a decision. Set a day to make the decision and decide which jobs you will apply for. It can be good to apply for more than one job, so you have a 'plan B', but keep the list small enough that you can put enough effort into each job application so that they reach a good standard.

Interviews

An interview can be the toughest part of getting a job, because you are being judged and may be anxious, which can make tics come out to play.

You
I hate to 'perform' in front of other people so the interview will be the most difficult part of getting a job for me.

Interviews can make you anxious, particularly about tics, so plan your interview responses to reduce stress

One month before

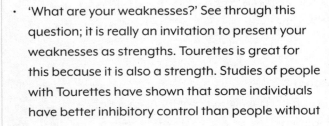

Dr Tara

Find answers to questions. Interviewers often ask people the same questions, so think about some good answers. Some common questions where Tourettes might come up are:

- 'What are your weaknesses?' See through this question; it is really an invitation to present your weaknesses as strengths. Tourettes is great for this because it is also a strength. Studies of people with Tourettes have shown that some individuals have better inhibitory control than people without

Tourettes, because they spend so much time practising stopping tics!

- 'How do you like to work – in a team or solo?' This one is often an attempt to find out if you have trouble getting on with people. The correct answer is always 'I am a natural team player, but am self-motivated enough to work on my own, where required.' Be careful not to depict Tourettes as an impediment to teamwork.

One week before

Zak

Practise interviews. Get someone to ask you questions, so you are used to interviews and get constructive feedback. Have people ask you unexpected questions, so you get used to thinking up good answers on the spot.

Dr Tara

Use a timer. Make sure you get used to modulating your tics for the correct time periods, and your answers are the right sort of length.

Megan

Use remote opportunities. If there is a chance to communicate via phone or email prior to the interview, use it, so the interviewer can form an opinion of your skills before being distracted by tics.

Tomorrow

Jobs

Zak

Plan your day to reduce stress. Make a mental timetable by thinking about how long each task takes and how much time you need between tasks. The goal is to be 'on autopilot' tomorrow, so you will only need to think about doing one task at a time.

Harry

Organise transport. It can be tough to hold your tics in on a bus journey and then all through an interview. Choose a transport option that gives you space to tic before and after the interview.

Today

Megan

Arrive early. Give yourself enough time that travel disruptions don't cause you anxiety.

Daniel

Focus on your strengths. It may be useful to mention your tics to the interviewer so your tics aren't interpreted as a lack of confidence. That said, make sure the interview is all about your strengths and aspirations, and not about your disorder.

Starting a new job

Your first day is when you get to know everyone and they get to know you – including your tics.

You

For me, the trickiest thing is the first day in any new place; after that I can usually manage well. I'm wondering if I should tell my co-workers about my tics as I start on the first day, or explain them when they happen.

One month before

Dr Tara

Find out the employment environment. If you know people at the job, ask them. Review websites like 'Glassdoor' can help you understand the company's culture.

One week before

Zak

Decide whether to tell co-workers. Before you get too close to the date, you should consider whether you will tell your future co-workers about Tourettes before you turn up. Telling everyone – letting people know about tics before you arrive – is a courteous thing to do and may be helpful if your tics are large or distracting. The downside is you could be 'that Tourettes guy' in everyone's mind.

Jess

Explain your particular tics. Whenever I meet somebody new I always explain that I have Tourettes, that they'll hear my most frequent tics, 'biscuit' and 'hedgehog', a lot, and that they can ask me if they have any questions. I also explain that my tics might intensify and that I might need to take a break. I tend to use the same words every time – it's now a normal part of how I introduce myself. It also means people have an opportunity to understand me, rather than worry about how to respond to my tics.

Megan

Not telling everyone avoids the troublesome first impressions. If your tics are mild or you work in a separate space, then maybe nobody will notice much. But working in close quarters with someone who has distracting tics and won't acknowledge it may be difficult for everyone.

Tomorrow

Harry
Prepare transport. Plan your transport route and make sure the train/bus route is running.

Today

Zak
Be early. Take a short walk when you get there to calm yourself and release any tics. Being early also gives you a margin in case transport goes wrong.

Everyday work

The main things to think about here are your co-workers and keeping yourself calm. Work can cause anxiety – especially if you worry that your tics might bother co-workers.

You
I've never worked in a proper office before and am worried that it's going to be even more difficult than a classroom or lecture theatre.

I'm particularly concerned about open plan spaces, as there's nowhere to hide.

This month

Megan

Think about co-workers. Start thinking about who your tics affect and how you can make their life easier. Don't be afraid to ask your boss or co-workers – most people are appreciative if you consider them. You might also find out they are not as bothered as you expected (see For other people → Employers).

Zak

Practise working under pressure. Stress can make your tics worse, so learn to handle pressure well (see Tools → Handling pressure).

Dr Tara

Practise tic control. If you get good enough at controlling tics that it becomes second-nature, then it is less of a drain on you at critical times (see Tools → Exposure and response prevention).

This week

jobs

Harry

Arrange things to suit your tics. If you're going to be in an office for a week, that's enough time to bother arranging things so that you don't distract others or don't hurt yourself when you tic.

Mike

Choose a discreet desk. At work, if I was in an open plan area, I liked to sit at the end rather than the middle, so that I didn't feel my colleagues were looking at me just by looking up. It meant I needed to put in a bit less effort not to tic while I was sitting at my desk. Of course, first prize is having your own office!

Dr Tara

Find a 'tic-friendly' location to work. Find a space where you can keep working when tics get bad. Be open to unusual locations, like a canteen or the car park, where noise is expected.

Jess

Make a tic space. Where I work I have space I can go to if my tics intensify – it's kitted out with mats and beanbags. I also have a support worker who types for me because my tics make this hard, and my working hours are flexible. These are all 'reasonable adjustments'.

Tomorrow

Zak

Experiment to remove tic triggers. Consider what you can do differently that reduces the urge to tic – anything from timing of the day to sitting position. Try changing one thing each day to find out what the source is. By the time you have changed everything, you'll have changed the job! (See Tools → Tic triggers.)

Harry

Tic 'weather warning'. If your tics are getting stronger, it might be fair to let other people know, so they can make allowances, like bringing headphones (if your tics are loud).

Today

Dr Tara

Work from home. If the tics are exceptionally frequent, loud or disruptive on a particular day, then see if you can work from home.

With clients or away off-site

Representing your company to clients and other people who are not used to your tics can be difficult because you want to give a good impression, but they may be unfamiliar with tics, or misinformed, and your usual workplace solutions aren't available.

> **You**
> Meeting new people is difficult for me even though after a few hours I can blend in well. Just the thought of it makes my tics explode. What can I do in new work spaces?

One month before

> **Dr Tara**
> *Practise similar tasks.* Do tasks similar to those you will be doing in your client's context, to build up a set of skills for managing the type of tics you will have there.

> **Zak**
> *Practise dealing with clients or customers.* The best people at dealing with clients or customers are confident, thoughtful and attentive. Tics make no difference to these skills, so develop these skills to the point you can just 'switch

them on'. To practise these skills, there are sales courses you can attend, or you can volunteer in places such as charity shops or libraries.

Jobs

Mike

Be confident. There is not a lot that confidence doesn't solve. If we are confident in our abilities, our hard work and our positive qualities, then tics become a minor consideration – just something that's in the back of our mind that we will control as best we can.

Dr Tara

Minimise face-to-face time. Many meetings only require you to be physically present for some of the time. You can often organise work so that large parts of it are done by phone, email or chat with video turned off. Don't eliminate too much 'people time' though; some face-to-face contact time is essential.

Mike

Control the tics you can. If you don't have verbal (complex vocal) tics, a job involving a lot of time on the phone means you can get a lot done without putting too much effort into controlling tics.

One week before

Megan

Introduce yourself. Contact people by email or phone before you meet them. It helps other people establish a rapport, so that in your first meeting tics are only a minor part of what they know about you.

Harry

Change focus. Arrange your work, presentation or pitch so it focuses on something other than yourself (e.g. a document or object).

Tomorrow

Zak

Arrange breaks. Organise your work so it has natural breaks in it, so you can get a drink of water and get rid of some tics. You may deliberately leave some things in a different room, to give yourself a reason to leave the room.

Dr Tara

Tag-team. If you are there with other people, plan for them to cover for you while you take a break.

Harry

Swoop in. I know that other people like to arrive early, but I usually plan to get there exactly on time. So you don't have time to stand around getting anxious. Momentum is an important part of the impression you need to make.

Today

Zak

Reduce anxiety. Anxiety makes tics worse, and makes you unhappy. If you have several hours to go, exercise to relax yourself (e.g. take a brisk walk). If you have less time, do breathing exercises (see Tools → Breathing and mindfulness).

Mike

Take time for yourself. If I am away at an event with colleagues and have been controlling tics all day, then I find it is very helpful to take an hour or two for myself after the work is done and before everyone gets together in the bar. Even if it is half an hour when I can relax, and even if it means missing the first round! I will also often go for a run, which is a great release.

jobs

Harry

Focus on your work, not tics. Tics often reduce when you focus, and people care more about your work than your tics, so make sure you focus on work.

Mike

Don't stress about tics. A few times I have chaired conferences of hundreds of people. There were video cameras on me the whole time, with the video streaming onto a huge screen behind me. I was a bit worried that everyone would sit and watch the giant me on the screen tic for three days! It was quite tiring putting in the effort not to tic, but most of the time I was concentrating very hard on chairing such a big meeting – and concentrating hard on other things helps a lot with tics. I know I used some rubbing of the eyes as a chance to sneak in some tics, but otherwise I honestly don't know how much I ticced. No one ever said anything to me – except to thank me for keeping the meeting on schedule and for getting the right result – so I guess I'll never know!

Dr Tara

Be attentive to your clients. Do they even notice your tics? You only need to break for tics that are disturbing clients, so be attentive to whether they are actually being distracted.

Megan

Don't try too hard to hide tics. People are good at spotting evasive behaviour, and it makes them distrustful. Better to be up-front and focused. In the end people want your goods or service, so focus on that, not tics.

jobs

Mike

Be creative with breaks. If I am at an event, I will sometimes get up and go and stand with the smokers outside and have a chat with them (as long as I can stand upwind!). It gives me an excuse to move and to have a break from the intensity of sitting still.

 Hanging out with co-workers

When you've been working with people for a while, some of them may invite you to a non-work occasion, like after-work drinks. Your workmates are used to handling your tics in one environment, but it can be quite different in other locations.

You

I'd really like to get to know the people I work with, but it's a bit scary.

One month before

Harry

Help choose the venue. Try to choose a place with enough background noise and activity that your tics won't stand out.

Megan

Ease them in. Take advantage of semi-work situations like lunchtimes to establish companionship and an 'outside of work' personality.

Dr Tara

Test out drinking (if you are old enough). Some people find that alcohol makes them tic more, others find it makes them tic less. It's good to find what alcohol does to your tics well before any event that has workmates. Be moderate – even if alcohol improves your tics, too much alcohol will make you much more embarassing than tics!

Tomorrow

Zak

Plan your day to reduce stress. Move chores and deadlines to another day, so you can relax and enjoy other people's company.

Harry

Sleep well. Tiredness increases tics more and decreases fun.

Today

Megan

Fit in. Most groups of people have well-established routines and roles. Learn what they are. Take it easy and try to fit in with how they do things.

Living with tics at home

You probably spend a lot of time at home, so it's important to think about how your tics affect you and other people there.

Why waste time watching tics?

Informal times

You

It's weird because although my family knows that I have tics and I relax at home, that's where most of my tics come out. I'm not sure why this is or how to talk to my parents about it.

This month

Harry

Prepare your home for tics. You can add padding on sharp corners to protect your body if you have a punching tic or similar.

Zak

Reduce triggers. Triggers are the things that make you tic or obsess (e.g. organising your book shelf). Try to find alternative objects that don't trigger tics in you (see Tools → Tic triggers).

This week

Megan

Get family support. Your family is a big part of your team. Get them on board for support (see For other people → Parents/ Family members).

Harry

Share information with your extended family.
Sometimes it's difficult for more distant
relatives to understand. Make sure you
try to talk to them and offer sensible information
about Tourettes.

Tomorrow

Mike

Take a break from controlling tics. I let myself off
the hook a bit when I am alone or with my wife
so I can get a good rest from controlling the
tics. However, apart from occasionally, I will still look
to control them at least a bit so that I avoid reinforcing
them too much.

Today

Harry

Remember to relax. Make sure you take time
for yourself to relax and spend time with
your family and friends. It's a good idea to
warn them that you are not planning to control your
tics during the activity and make any arrangements
needed for this (see For other people → Friends).

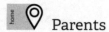 ## Parents

> **You**
> My parents want to help, but they keep commenting on my tics, which makes things worse. What can I do?

This month

Dr Tara

Help your parents help you. Parents wanting to help is a good thing. However, there is one golden rule for your parents. You need to train them to get used to ignoring your tics. Parents who think that constantly commenting on your tics will be helpful are mistaken.

Zak

Show your parents sensible and official information on their role in tic management. Any sensible book (including this one – see For other people → Parents) will guide parents to ignore tics. However, if you want to talk about tics with your parents they should find time to discuss them in private.

Megan

Speak with your parents. Tell them about how you would like them to respond when you tic. This is different for everyone with tics and their particular parents.

Dr Tara

If your parent has tics, discuss this with them. If one of your parents has had tics, see if they are happy to discuss this with you. It's likely that you'll be able to learn from one another.

This week

Zak

Show your parents how well you cope. Your parents and family are likely to worry about you. If you can show them how well you manage your life, school, job, relationships and hobbies, this will benefit everyone.

Megan

Be understanding. It's likely that your parents may feel uncertain or even guilty about you having tics, so be gentle with them.

Tomorrow

Harry

Observe your parents. See how and when your parents comment on tics or look at you when you tic. Make a note of how you best like them to react, so they know what would be helpful, and more comfortable.

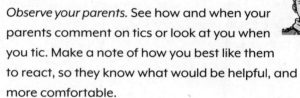

Today

Dr Tara

Answer questions. The chances are that you are an expert on tics because you have them and because you have read at least some of this Survival Kit. Ask your parents if they have any particular questions, and help them to be experts too!

Mike

When you discuss tics, it is different for everyone. I never discussed Tourettes with my parents. There was no information available at school or elsewhere, so when I first developed tics I had to figure it out myself. It's great that these days there is generally more discussion and more information.

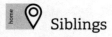 Siblings

Siblings can be your biggest allies in surviving with Tourettes, or your biggest challenge.

You
Although we get on about most things pretty well, my tics drive my brother crazy.

This month

Harry
Model ignoring behaviour. In public, siblings ignore your tics because they are used to them. Let others see that people familiar with tics ignore them, so they know to do the same.

Megan
Stand up for you. Siblings often stand up for you because they don't like to see other people making fun of your tics. Include them in your support crew (see For other people → Family members).

This week

Zak

Relax. Some siblings will use anything they can find to wind you up. Your survival challenge here is not to get worked up. Would you get worked up if someone teased you for having five fingers? Of course not! Tourettes is like that – just a natural part of who you are.

Harry

Explain to your sibling. People who are shy about asking you directly will often ask your siblings about the tics they see. Train your siblings on what to say – that tics are very common and nothing to worry about.

Tomorrow

Harry

Figure out how to avoid annoying things siblings do. Most siblings do things that annoy you – either accidentally or deliberately – and can provoke anxiety or trigger tics. Work out how to avoid these triggers.

Jess

Discuss tricky situations. I talk to my friends and family about situations that I find tricky; they'll often help me work out what to do or what to say.

Today

Zak

Be nice to your siblings. They can be your strongest defence and you will have them with you for a long time.

 Getting a pet

Pets don't understand tics, but they get used to them pretty fast and can be a huge help in making you feel relaxed and happy.

You

I'd like to get a pet but am not sure about what kind of animal will be relaxed around my tics.

One month before

home

Megan

Research the type of pet. There are some pets that don't go well with some tics, so if you have big motor tics, then maybe a fragile pet isn't the best pet to choose. Look online and talk to breeders/vets/staff at the pound about an animal. Think carefully about how you would handle the animal at home – does it like petting? How often does it need to be groomed or cleaned?

Harry

Choose the pet. It might be helpful to go along and visit the animal before you make up your mind about getting it. Choose a pet that likes you, doesn't seem affected by your tics and suits your energy.

One week before

Dr Tara

Practical plans. Make sure you have a bed and feeding plate for the animal. Have you thought about how you might bring the pet home and cope with any excitement-provoked tics? Will the animal be able to sleep in your bedroom or will it need a bed and area of its own? How will it cope with loud vocal tics?

Zak

Planning care of the animal. Discuss with your family or flatmates about who will be looking after the pet. Is it realistic that you will be able to care for the pet all of the time, or will you need help?

Tomorrow

Harry

Make a decision to get the pet. Push the button.

Today

Megan

Relax and enjoy. Animals are sensitive creatures, so relax once you get your pet and he or she will know that they are wanted.

 Visitors

When you're used to not controlling your tics at home, having a visitor around can be hard work. Visitors aren't used to seeing tics, and you might be anxious not to upset them, because they haven't learned to ignore tics.

You

Home is usually a relaxing place for me and my tics, but they often increase if we have visitors coming over. What can I do?

One week before

Harry

Try to find your current triggers. Figure out which situations make you tic the most when visitors are over, so you know where you will need to use strategies (see Tools → Tic triggers).

Megan

Plan a place where you can release your tics. Find a place where you can tic without worrying about being seen or heard.

Mike

Take breaks. During dinner parties I take a break from the effort of controlling tics by getting up to clear the table and taking plates through to the kitchen. Then cleaning up a bit in the kitchen from time to time. No one ever complains! I am also very good at getting up to fetch more drinks, or just to leave the room every now and then if I feel like it. At other people's houses I am quick to help clear the table so I can move around, which means I quickly become a very popular guest!

Tomorrow

Harry

Let your visitor know if your tics are big. Hopefully your visitor may already know about your tics. If they do, just send them a quick message to prepare them if the tics are severe currently. If it's news to them that you have tics, perhaps a quick phone call could be useful from you or a member of the family to help them to be prepared and cope well (see Tools → For other people).

Today

Zak

Use your toolkit. Do some exercises to relax you, then allow yourself some space to get your tics out of the way before the visitor arrives. Tic suppress if this helps you (see Tools → Suppressing tics).

Holidays

Holidays can be a strange mix, because you are with your family who are used to tics, but surrounded by strangers who may never have seen tics before.

You

New places are often triggers for my tics, particularly holidays, but I do love getting a break and seeing new places.

One month before

Dr Tara

Be prepared. Planning ahead for a holiday will be helpful. Look up on the internet where you will be staying and get familiar with it. Research what resources and activities are going to be available at your holiday destination.

One week before

Megan

Make a list. Know the equipment to bring with you. Remember to bring your letter or cards that say that you have Tourettes.

Tomorrow

Harry

Sort tics on transport. Plan how you will manage your tics while on public transport. The chances are that you will be very excited about going on holiday, which may increase the tics (see Situations → Public transport).

Today

Zak

Use your tic management. Use your tic suppression, competing responses, exercise and relaxation strategies to manage tics. Most of all, enjoy yourself! (See Tools → Living with Tourettes.)

 Getting into trouble

Part of growing up is learning the boundaries, and part of exploring the boundaries is finding yourself on the wrong side of the rules, sometimes.

You

Sometimes I just cannot control my mouth. What can I do?

This month

Megan

Make a safety margin. When you were very young, people gave you a lot of slack, but now that you are a young adult, you are responsible for staying inside the rules. The trouble is, Tourettes can push you over the line a bit. If you're in a delicate situation, then a vocal or motor tic might be the last straw. This means you need to be a bit more careful than everyone else, and a bit more skilled at staying out of trouble. A safety margin means leaving enough space between you and the rules, that a tic won't push you over the line.

Harry

Figure out who can help you. In the movies, when someone is arrested, they are allowed one phone call. Who would your phone call be to? Find someone who will bail you out of trouble if a person in authority wants to see a 'responsible adult' about your behaviour.

Zak

Choose your friends carefully. Some people get into more trouble than others. When choosing which of your friends to hang out with, try to choose ones who get their kicks a little further away from the law's boundary (e.g. choose rock climbing instead of Parkour).

This week

Dr Tara

Prepare an explanation. To uninformed people, tics can look like misbehaviour or drunkenness, so it's useful to have an explanation ready (see For other people → Officials).

Tomorrow

Megan
Pack this book. The back of this book has
ready-made explanations for when your tics
get you in trouble (see For other people).

Today

Zak
Let other people test the boundaries. If your
friends are doing things that might get you
into trouble, take a step back to give yourself
some margin. Tourettes affects your body, not your
sight or sense.

First dates and beyond with tics
Getting your game on

A big part of being a young adult may be having a
romantic or sexual partner, but there is a big step to
learn between wanting a relationship and having one.

You
I worry that it's going to be difficult for
someone to see beyond my tics when they first
meet me.

love

Tell the person you like early; don't worry

One month before

Harry

Let the world know. The first step is usually letting the world know that you're looking. Get dressed up, hang out in places with other young single people and put yourself out there. Tics don't change this at all – you still need to 'see' and 'be seen'.

Megan

Become yourself. Just like having straight or curly hair, Tourettes is a part of the story of who you are. Tourettes may make you zany, and your friends will riff off that, enjoying the spice it brings.

One week before

Megan

Have fun. Most of your game is being 'on form', so just make sure you hang out with people who make you happy. When you are 'on form', your tics seem part of who you are, not some separate force to struggle with.

love

Tomorrow

Zak

Get some sleep. Going out when you are tired makes it harder to control tics (see Tools → Sleep).

Today

Harry

Decide where to go out. When you go out with friends you usually think about where is popular and entertaining, where the best people are and where the transport is good. Tourettes is just one more factor in that choice – so if you have vocal tics, maybe you will go to a loud venue rather than a quiet one.

Mike

Be cunning. Places like the university library or canteen can be great for keeping an eye on the social scene. Sitting off to the side where you can see someone you like, but they can only see you if they turn, means it's easier to know when to put in the effort of controlling the tics. Otherwise, sitting in their direct line of sight for a couple of hours can be very hard work!

Meeting people

You

Just hanging out isn't going to cut it; I need to meet new people. I need to make an excuse to speak to them, without my tics getting in the way.

Harry

Tourettes is your secret weapon, because it's a natural ice-breaker.

This month

Dr Tara

Try to cultivate more than one group of friends. Maybe you have one group of friends you study or socialise with and another you do sport with or play games with? Having more groups of friends lets you meet new people often, and is good practice at getting you used to other people who don't think like you.

Zak

Be open to opportunities. Hanging out with one friend often leads to hanging out with their other friends.

Megan

Get online – carefully. Another way to meet people is online. People can get to know a bit about you before they see your tics, which can help you gain confidence. But people's online persona is usually different from their real-life persona, so people who seem great online can sometimes just not work out in reality. Purely online romance isn't fulfilling, so make sure that your online world is plugged into your offline one. Online dating or meet-ups can be a colourful place to meet people, giving you access to many more people than your social circle, and letting you find 'like-minded' people. But be careful – some dating apps can be unsafe, and some carry an expectation of a quick-fix of intimacy without romance, that will ultimately leave you unsatisfied, like junk food. A good place to start meeting people online is choosing the platform. What platform offers the type of opportunity you are looking for?

Zak

Decide whether Tourettes is in your profile. Most dating forums need you to make a profile, so a big question is whether you put Tourettes on your profile. The right answer depends on you – putting Tourettes in your profile could put some people off contacting you, but leaving it out will mean some dates will be more awkward. The answer mostly depends on how frequent/loud/large/controllable your tics are and how appealing the rest of your profile is – if you look like a fashion model and have too many date requests, then saying you have Tourettes might help narrow down people beyond the superficial. If you're not getting many dates, then leaving Tourettes off your profile gives people a chance to meet you first and see what tics really are, before making a decision.

love

Mike

Dating is tricky for everyone. It's possible someone decided not to date me because I had Tourettes, but then people decide these things based on the totality of whether someone is attractive to them or not. I'm sure I was also turned down by someone because of the length and colour of my hair, and someone else for the clothes I wear. The reality is that we will be turned down sometimes, no matter what!

This week

Megan

Gather topics. Spend some time thinking about interesting aspects of your life and interests you could speak about on a date. This could be hobbies, where you go to school or college, friends, current affairs or even background information on Tourettes. The more prepared you are the better a conversationalist you will be and your date will be able to see how interesting and even funny you are.

Dr Tara

Be slow to judge people. Most people have an interesting story behind them, but just aren't very good at presenting or describing themselves. Just as you would rather people didn't judge you only on Tourettes, make sure you don't just assess someone else on the first things they say or their first reaction to your tics.

Tomorrow

Harry

Test chat with yourself. Sometimes it's helpful to talk to yourself or think over what topics you might like to discuss with people in your own mind.

Today

Zak
Fake it to make it. Sometimes you just have to put yourself in the situation and make it happen, even when you are nervous.

 Letting someone know you are interested

You
Having a crush on someone doesn't get me anywhere. Sooner or later I need to let them know I am interested. I'm nervous because of the fear of being turned down, and tics can make it harder.

This month

Megan
Try to spend time near the person. Arrange events so opportunities to be near the person you like arise. They can't like you if they don't know you!

This week

Dr Tara
One-on-one time. Plan an activity that will give you a moment alone with them; choose an activity that tics won't interrupt.

Tomorrow

Harry
Ask your friends to help. Having a 'wingman' who can help you create the perfect moment is a huge help.

Today

Zak
Make a 'sign'. You needn't wait for the other person to provide an opportunity. Catch that person's eye, and see if they respond.

Harry
Look out for a sign. Often someone will drop you hints that they are interested, such as catching your eye or sharing a smile. Beyond that, they may create a situation that gives you an opportunity to approach them, such as taking a walk alone to get drinks, or mingling with your circle of

friends and engaging. You usually only get one sign, so stay alert. Be gracious if you've misread the sign.

Megan

Make a move. Say 'hi'. Invite the person to an event. It's not a big deal if they say 'no'. The timing isn't always right, and even rock stars get turned down. Also, if it isn't going to happen, isn't it better to know now than spend weeks wondering? Often there is no good time to ask, just worse times, so grab hold of fate and try today.

First date

You

A first date makes me nervous. Neither of us knows what to expect – will we click or not? Tics can increase that nervousness, and nervousness can increase tics. What can I do to stop feeling so nervous and ticcy?

This month

Zak

Practise tic suppression. You only really need to hold your tics in a few minutes for the first impression. Practise tic suppression tools until you get good enough that your date can see you smile comfortably. There's no point holding tics in, if it makes you grimace and squirm with the effort! (See Tools → Living with Tourettes.)

This week

Dr Tara

Safety. On your first date you will be spending time with someone you don't know well and may have no previous experience of tics. Try to find a 'chain of trust', someone you both know in common that you trust. Look for some proof that your date really is who they say they are (e.g. friends in common or social media profile). Tell a friend or parent who your date is, where you will go, and when you expect to be back, and make sure that person can be trusted to raise an alert if you don't check in.

Zak

Gain familiarity. The more you know a person or place, the less anxious you become. Ask someone who knows your date what they like. Spend some time in the area you will be going out, so you know where is good, and some of the little magic corners.

Harry

Plan it. Where will you go? Where will you go after that? Have a plan A and plan B, so you can change depending on what they want. The aim is to look clever and spontaneous, not over-planned and controlling.

love

Megan

Think of an idea for a second date. If the first date is going well, you may want to ask them to do something else with you. It's great to have something already in mind, so you don't have to rack your brains during the date. Offering an intriguing adventure sounds much more inviting than 'Do you want to do something else some time?'

Tomorrow

Megan

Prepare. Think about what you will wear, what you will be doing and the impression you want to make. Heels are good for cocktail bars but not the beach.

Zak

Think about transport. Give yourself options to leave early or late, depending on how well it goes. If you are using public transport, be aware of when the final transport departs.

Today

Dr Tara

Smile. People like other people who smile. They like to think they made you smile, so make your smiles happen in response to something they did or said.

Zak

Be easy-going. Wanting something too much is unattractive, so relax and allow the date to work. If your chemistry is right, then relaxing helps you click (and if it's not right, then better to find out now than spend many dates trying to force it).

Mike

Controlling tics is up to you. At the start of a relationship it makes sense to put a lot of effort into controlling tics. Over time it gets easier to relax the level of effort to some extent as you get to know each other better. Relationships end for all kinds of reasons and it's very unlikely that Tourettes will be one of them!

Second dates and beyond

> **You**
> Second dates are when you truly get to know what someone is like. How can I make me and my tics easy to spend time with?

One week before

> **Zak**
> *Practise manners.* A lot of being in a relationship with someone is the gaps between activities, when you negotiate who does what. Most of that negotiation is done with manners, like taking turns to speak, respecting the other person's opinion and personal space (unless they indicate otherwise), and focusing on them instead of yourself.

> **Megan**
> *Arrange another date.* Don't leave it too long between your first and second date. People are not single forever, and you are trying to build on the impression you made in the first date, not start from scratch again!

love

Zak

Share interests. Find out what interests you have in common. Don't be afraid to try something you've never done before – one of the great things about relationships is they widen the activities you've tried.

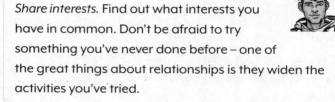

Harry

Help them get used to tic attention. Show the other person how to respond with strangers noticing tics (you're used to people staring, but your boyfriend/girlfriend might not be).

Dr Tara

Ask the other person if any of your tics are particularly challenging for them. For example, this could be a repetitive sniff that could be frustrating for a person who spends a lot of time with you. Talk with them and hear what they say and think about how the situation can be changed.

Harry

Think about whether or not you like talking about your tics with that person. Let them know. If they are curious and have questions that you don't want to discuss, then give them this Survival Kit.

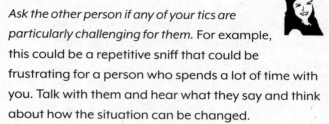

Tomorrow

Zak
The most important thing in a second date is to be yourself.

Dr Tara
Think of some topics to talk about. It's better to arrive armed with some topics you think are interesting, that you can introduce at the right time to avoid awkward silences.

Zak
Be open to intimacy. This doesn't necessarily mean physical intimacy, but be prepared to let a person into your world a little bit, so they can see your perspective.

Today

Harry
Model ignoring tics. If you ignore your tics, then soon they will too.

Mike
Remember people's priorities. In a relationship, things like kindness, respect and humour are

a lot more important to the other person than whether you tic.

 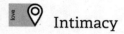 ## Intimacy

You

Being intimate and physical with another person can be scary for anyone. Having tics to cope with makes me even more nervous. What can I do?

This month

Zak

Don't worry. Most people with tics don't have problems with intimacy. Even people with severe tics usually don't say that intimacy is a problem. Early physical relationships are a bit awkward. It's likely that the other person will also be nervous.

Harry

Chat with someone. Choose someone you know well who can reassure you and give you ideas if you're not certain about what might happen.

Zak

Find solutions to tic issues. If your tics could cause injury, discomfort or even just break the mood, then start thinking about how you can avoid those issues. Most people find tics don't interfere with intimacy, but the most important thing is to make sure the other person is not in harm's way.

Mike

Intimacy might help tics. Moments of intimacy are intense, and an intense focus on anything limits tics a lot.

This week

Zak

Choose where you might get intimate with someone. Choose a place where your tics won't be as much of a problem and you are safe. Perhaps this could be a time to discuss with your parents and see if they might be okay with you being at home with someone you are dating.

Tomorrow

Harry

Assess how your tics are today. See what plans you need to change, while there is still time.

Today

Zak
Look after everything else. There is not much you can do about tics at this stage, so make sure everything else is ready. Make sure you are well groomed and in the mood.

Dr Tara
Play nice. Being respectful and kind both to yourself and whoever you are with is key, and anything that follows from there will be fine.

Zak
Go at your own pace. Intimacy can start small and grow quickly or slowly, so go at a pace that you enjoy and enables you to be yourself in all areas, including how you manage tics together. Maybe it's time to share more tailored information on Tourettes (see For other people → Girlfriends/ boyfriends).

 Meeting your date's friends and family

You
We've had a few good dates and now she wants me to meet her friends and family. I'm

terrified (especially of her parents), and wonder what they will think of me and my tics.

One month before

Mike

Focus on being good. Parents don't lie awake at night worrying about their son or daughter being out with someone with Tourettes. They lie awake at night worrying about whether their son or daughter is out with someone who will look after them, be kind to them, and make them happy.

Mike

Make an effort initially. I always make a strong effort to control tics when meeting new people. Beyond that, if they see me tic, then so be it – if I'm going to be in a relationship with someone, then their friends and family will probably at some point realise that this is part of me anyway.

One week before

Megan

Practise conversation strategies. You can use strategies for developing conversation.

Tomorrow

Dr Tara
Be ready to explain about tics to the family.
Rehearse the sorts of sensible facts that you
might want to share with your date's parents,
siblings or extended family (see Tools → Helpers).

Today

Megan
Be your best self. Show the interesting, funny
and caring side of you to your partner's family.
This will be the most important aspect of
getting to know them.

Mike
Be more than tics. Your new partner's family
will be looking for signs that you are a decent
person who will treat their son/daughter/
brother/sister with kindness and generosity, and them
with respect. If you get that part right, then they won't
be worrying about a few tics.

Driving and other important tasks

Driving and tests

Driving equals freedom for a lot of people. Having tics does not automatically stop you from driving although you may need to do more preparation than your friends before you get started.

You

I've been waiting to drive since I was four years old, and now that my tics are still strong at 17, I'm worried that I might not be allowed to drive like my friends.

This month

Dr Tara

Know the rules. Some tics can interfere with driving. It's important to be sure of what the rules are in your country. Look up the 'road rules' on your local government website, and look at your country's Tourettes support site to see if they have any information about tics and driving.

Megan

Get a permission letter. Discuss this with your doctor or specialist, who should be able to give you advice and write an authorising letter.

Get a letter of consent from your doctor

Zak

Contact your driving regulation organisation.
Call, email or look on the website of your national driving regulation organisation to find out if they should know about your diagnosis of Tourettes. You can be fined if you apply for a licence and do not declare the information.

Megan

Find a good teacher. If a driving school is how you will learn to drive, then contact several driving instructors to see who understands (or is willing to learn) about your tic-related challenges. If someone you know is going to teach you, then have an honest chat with them about how your tics can impact you in a car and how you cope with it (see For other people → Teachers/Lecturers).

driving

This week

Dr Tara

Get your paperwork. Make sure that you have your learner licence ready, including the sight test result and anything else you might need.

Zak

Rules of the road. Look over the relevant website, app or book to review the rules of the road.

Megan

Watch others. While you are driving with other people, watch what they do and how they drive. Remember you will be driving while managing your tics.

Dr Tara

Sit behind the wheel. Sit in the driver's seat without turning the key in the ignition. A little 'off-line' practice might be helpful before you actually turn the engine on.

driving

Duncan

Know which tics you can control. There are certain tics, like taking the steering wheel and whipping it to the side while going 90 miles an hour, that I know will cause an accident and I know it will probably kill me. It's like the survivalist instincts take over and say, 'I don't care how much you want to scratch that itch, you're not going to do it. End of story.'

Tomorrow

Dr Tara

Plan it out. Organise your driving lesson or test and make sure you have plenty of time. Think about how you will manage your tics.

Today

Zak

Use your best tic management. Do some exercises to relax you, then allow yourself some space to get your tics out of the way before the examiner arrives. Tic suppress if this helps you, but remember to keep focused on your lesson or test (see Tools → Immediate help).

Daniel

Only drive if safe. Do not feel any shame in avoiding driving if your tics are impairing your ability. You wouldn't push yourself to drive with a broken leg, and tics are no different. The most important thing is to stay safe.

driving

driving

Operating equipment

You

I need to operate equipment sometimes, like sharp knives, a Bunsen burner or a bicycle pump. Other people get worried about me doing things and using equipment – usually I'm fine, but I would like to be sure.

This month

Dr Tara

Take simple precautions. Tics can play havoc with equipment, so it's advisable to take some simple precautions relevant to your tics. Just because you don't feel a tic coming on doesn't mean you are safe, so figure out what would happen if you ticced before starting to use the equipment.

Zak

Make some space. You might want to look at the amount of free space you have around the activity and decide if you can control the size of motor tics around the equipment you are working on.

Jess

Tourettes-proof it. I have 'Tourettes-proofed' my house; for me this means that kitchen knives are kept covered and out of sight, there are mats and cushions around for when I need them and I use camping cups that have lids so I get less wet when I drink. These simple adjustments have made me much safer and more independent.

Harry

Wear protective clothing. This could be a cycle helmet, gloves or elbow pads. This can help you or other people close by, so long as the equipment doesn't endanger people's lives.

Megan

Try moving activities into the 'safe zone'.
Tourettes isn't entirely uncontrolled – you can avoid some compulsions (e.g. while driving). See if you can move other unsafe activities into that 'safe zone' by focusing, being very careful when doing them, or doing them a different way?

This week

Zak

Discuss your tics. If other people are nearby you or involved in the activity, it's a good idea to discuss your tics with them so that they can prepare in any way they need to.

driving

Tomorrow

Harry

Test it out. It's hard to know in advance what tasks will give you problems with tics. Some tasks you think might be problematic turn out to be fine, while others are surprisingly difficult. Arrange test runs without risk to other people. Do as many test runs as you need to be sure there won't be a problem.

Zak

Assess the consequences. Take the time to figure out what could go wrong. If it's just you at risk, you may find the risk acceptable (e.g. using a drill) or be able to constrain things to keep safe (e.g. by cycling in the park on the grass and wearing padding). If other people are involved, you need to carefully communicate potential consequences to them, because they need to choose their own risk level.

Today

driving

Megan

Choose your tasks. If your tics are misbehaving on a particular day, then it might be worth deferring physically responsible tasks (like holding the bottom of a ladder for someone), particularly high-risk (involving fire, heights or electricity) or low-safety situations (like using knives). If you're not sure, discuss it with another person, or leave the task to someone else.

Dr Tara

Give your tics time to subside. Often, people find that after a period of time they are able to go to places and do things that they could not manage before due to tics. It's sensible to consider how risky a situation is depending on your current tics.

Megan

Whistle while you work. The strategy of using focused activities such as singing or tapping while doing tic-triggering activities might be helpful to try, although it is unlikely to work in every situation.

transit ⦿ Public transport

Public transport can be tough with tics, because you are stuck in a small space with strangers for a long time, so it may be too long a time to control tics. Travelling exposes your tics to the public – many people for a short time, and some people for a long time.

⦿ transit

transit ⦿ Travelling with tics

You

For me, the worst places are trains, planes and automobiles. They definitely make me more stressed and my tics come out to play. I'd like to reduce the impact of tics and still get around.

This month

Megan

Learn to handle nosiness. People are naturally socially interested – we want to look at each other, but in most cultures it is rude to be *too* socially interested. Most nosiness is solved by confronting it with a simple explanation, so it is helpful to practise explaining tics clearly and calmly to other people. Keep doing it until it comes naturally and confidently (see Tools → Explaining your tics to other people).

transit

Dr Tara

Get good at handling stressful situations.
Travelling involves stressful situations,
like getting there on time, having the
right ticket, handling luggage and hoping there is
space for you. Stress can provoke tics, so if you're
anxious about ticcing, it can be useful to have some
strategies to avoid stressful situations (see Tools →
Stress management).

This week

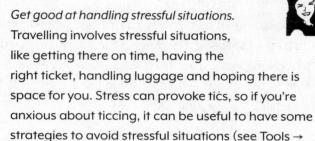

Zak

Choose the best form of transport. There may
be several different public transport options
to choose from such as the train, bus or taxi.
Most people choose their transport based on a variety
of factors like price, speed, convenience and reliability.
Tics are just another factor to add. Some types of
transport are more friendly to tics than others. Seats
that make you face each other can be difficult because
you are always under scrutiny. Transport that has
rigorous security like airports can be suspicious of tics
and cause anxiety. Personal transport such as driving
a car, walking or cycling can give you space away
from other people and provide exercise, which can
help reduce tics.

Jess

Get disabled transport privilege. I have a disabled person's railcard, which means I get discounted tickets for me and for another person to travel with me. Being able to travel with someone else is essential for my safety and comfort.

transit

Harry

Travel with someone else. Consider travelling with a friend or colleague because that normalises things for strangers – if your travelling companion seems undisturbed by your tics, then it's clear to other people that there is nothing to worry about.

Dr Tara

Choose the best time. Different people travel at different times – business people commute at peak times. If there is one type of person who is more troubled by tics when you travel, then travelling at different times can avoid them.

Tomorrow

Zak

Get it right in your head. How much you tic can depend on your state of mind, so it makes sense to try to make sure you feel calm and less ticcy. Taking time for exercise and mindfulness helps. You can also work on reducing anxiety, by preparing things in advance, giving yourself lots of time and by focusing on the activity and goal, rather than the worries.

Megan

Choose the right appearance. If you look respectable, it's easier to convince people that you are not crazy and living in a cave. Taking care of personal appearance helps reassure people that despite your tics breaking some rules, you manage to obey other rules, so are safe to share transport with. Conformity isn't the only option. Dressing differently, in a friendly but interesting way, can invite people to look at your clothes rather than your tics, and can say, 'Hey, I'm different but the world needs colour.'

Harry

Wait well. Waiting is often the hardest part because it makes people anxious (nobody wants to miss their transport) and gives people time to worry. Anxiety increases tics, and waiting can be a difficult time for ticcing because there is nothing else to look at except each other. Practise waiting in public places without needing something or someone to entertain you.

Megan

Reduce anxiety. Travelling can make us anxious, because flying, floating and rolling are not natural ways for people to move around. We are stuck in an enclosed space with strangers, and must trust them not to disturb or harm us. Walking down the street is more dangerous than flying (in a plane), but we fear flying more. Because anxiety about travel isn't rational, we need to be careful not to let it control us.

transit

Today

Dr Tara

Deal with officials. Most public transport has officials, and part of their job is to look out for behaviour that could cause trouble. Unfortunately many tics fit that description, so officials might take an interest in you. Officials may not be familiar with tics, so they might think giving you extra attention is part of their job. You need to expect that this will happen and always be ready with an explanation. Practise giving a calm description of what tics are and that you are allowed to travel. If you have an official document of disability, present that (see For other people → Officials).

Megan

Reduce staring. There are some ways to stop people staring at you while you wait:

- Face away from people, towards the direction that your transport will arrive from. Most people are more concerned about missing their stop than looking at each other. Stand at the back of the crowd.

- Stand away from the crowd. If there is a crowd waiting to board transport, you don't need to be around them, controlling your tics. Go somewhere a bit further away where you can relax.

- Tell the staring person that you have Tourettes, say it loudly enough that other people will hear your conversation, and be tactful.

Zak

Obey the rules. There are many 'good manners' rules about how we should act on public transport, like not yelling or physically disturbing other people, offering seats to elderly people, queuing without pushing and sitting still without fidgeting. Tics make it hard to follow some of the rules, so we need to make a new 'pact' with the people we travel with. Instead of our actions saying 'We both know the rules and will obey them', our body language has to say 'Although I can't obey all the rules, I will try my best and will ensure that you are always safe.' Those actions are:

- Tell people that you can't obey the usual social rules ('Please don't mind if I twitch my arm, I have Tourettes').

- Demonstrate that you are making an effort to keep to the rules (obey all the rules you can, and make an effort on the rules you can't).

- Be clear with people about the safety space you need ('Don't worry, tics are not contagious, I just need a bit of extra space for my elbow when it twitches'). Your fellow travellers may never have heard of tics, so they rely on you to demonstrate that you are treating their safety seriously.

transit

Jess

Talk about tics. Buses and other forms of transport that are quite enclosed and where people are usually quiet can feel really uncomfortable if you have tics. If people look worried or are clearly laughing at me, I will talk to them about Tourettes. This approach has led to lots of really interesting conversations. If somebody's behaving in a way that's unacceptable, I know I can go and tell the driver or another member of staff.

Dr Tara

Handle difficult people. You may come across people who comment on or who are curious about your tics. However, some behaviours can go beyond curiosity and can be rude, such as talking loudly about your tics or imitating your tics. This is not acceptable and you can ask the person to stop. If they do not, seek help from an official on the plane, train or bus. It's important not to become aggressive or overly confrontational, but keeping calm and being assertive and direct is key (see Tools → Hinderers). Your primary concern is security, so if it looks unsafe to confront the offending people, then it is best to avoid them.

Jess

It's okay to say 'no'. Sometimes when I'm travelling on my own and people just hear my tics I'll make a phone call to a friend so that those around me can hear my chosen words as well as the involuntary ones. This seems to help them relax a bit. People on public transport have sometimes filmed me, and I always find this incredibly upsetting. I ask the person to stop and make them delete the video. You don't have to put up with someone filming if it makes you uncomfortable.

Getting special accommodations

You

There are travel accommodations for people with disabilities. Can I get any for my Tourettes?

One month before

Harry

Get a doctor's letter. You may need a letter from your doctor or evidence of a disability that shows that you are entitled to disability adjustments.

transit

Dr Tara

Find what accommodations are available for your transport method. Accommodations are available for many transport types, so if you need them, make sure you ask for them when booking, as most accommodations need to be booked ahead of time. Look online before your trip and establish what you are entitled to ask for, and who you can complain to if they fail to provide it for you. A rough guide of what you can expect is:

- *Planes:* Boarding at a different time, understanding from the staff, and possibly additional space.

- *Trains:* Mobility assistance getting on the train; some even offer a mentoring service, in which you are accompanied during your first few uses of the service.

- *Buses/trams:* Buses offer mobility assistance and the ability to discuss your needs with the driver when you board.

transit

- *Taxis:* Select a company that you can get to know and use them when needed.

- *Ride share:* Ride share schemes often place you in a car with many other people; if you find people on a noticeboard or forum, be clear on what your needs are from the start.

- *Ferries:* Usually there is plenty of space on ferries; let the company know when you book about your needs and keep a copy of any emails or letters you exchange with them so you have this information to hand when you board the boat and make your journey.

Jess

Ask for assistance. Most airlines ask if you have any access requirements when you book – I always tell them that I have Tourettes. There are special assistance teams in most airports who can help you go through security more smoothly.

Zak

Make it safe. If you have tics that could endanger others (e.g. large arm tics) or yourself (e.g. eye poking), it is important that you explain during booking what space and equipment is needed to make it safe for you to travel. Your doctor's letter could specify what you need to travel safely.

Tomorrow

Megan

Choose where to sit. Some forms of transport let you choose your seat in advance. Choosing a seat is especially useful for people with Tourettes because it lets you choose a seat at the back where people will not see you ticcing, or a seat in the aisle that lets you get up often to relax without disturbing people. If you have large motor tics, then choose a seat that has space around it (e.g. near the toilet) so you won't disturb others.

transit

Today

Harry

Find space. Some seating locations are better than others for tics. If you have vocal tics, choose a noisy place, like near the engine, so your tics don't stand out so much. If you have motor tics, a seat near the back can be useful, so everyone is not looking at you. Standing up may also help because it gives you freedom to turn away from other people to hide tics, or to disguise tics with movement. Avoid places that are too isolated; remember that troublemakers choose the back seat of the bus for the same reason you do – to avoid scrutiny.

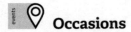 ## Occasions

There are a few life situations that are particularly worth thinking about and planning for.

 ### Special occasions (weddings, funerals, etc.)

You

I need to attend a one-off occasion that is important to a person I know and care about. Usually everyday life with tics is fine, but I think a lot about the 'big stuff', weddings, speeches... How can I stop my tics ruining the occasion?

One month before

Megan

Remind them. It's likely that whoever is organising the wedding has put a great deal of thought, effort and planning into the wedding. They will most likely know about your tics. If you have loud or disruptive tics, then it's helpful to remind the bride, groom or organiser about the sorts of tics you have and understand how you might cope on the wedding day.

events

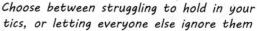

Choose between struggling to hold in your tics, or letting everyone else ignore them

Dr Tara

Make contact. Contact the venue of the wedding ceremony and reception to understand what adaptations can be made to support you in coping with your tics.

One week before

Harry

Practise behavioural therapy. It might be helpful to think about using competing responses to help contain any particularly bothersome tics you may have (see Tools → Behavioural therapy).

Tomorrow

Megan

Assess your tics. See how much coping and use of strategy you may have to do with your tics.

Today

Harry

Develop allies. Before the ceremony, everyone is getting to know each other. Find some people who don't mind your tics.

Megan

Speak with the celebrant or organiser. Explain if you have any motor or vocal tics that may be bothersome or stand out.

Dr Tara

Be brave. Explain to people that you have tics, if it feels right to do so (see Tools → Socialising).

Harry

Stand at the back. During ceremonies and speeches, everyone's attention is on the front, not the audience, so stand at the back if you are able.

Jess

Don't worry. During my sister's wedding I ticced a lot, including shouting about my brother-in-law's eyebrows during the vows. But I never felt worried about this because I knew I was welcome, and that my tics are part of the deal. This made their wedding much more memorable and full of laughter than it might otherwise have been.

 events

Zak

Beware emotional speeches. Speeches can be quite emotional and sometimes this can interact with people's tics. Be aware of this and make the necessary adjustments.

Daniel

Make some space for yourself. If you need to step outside for a minute during important events, then do. Even if people notice, they won't care.

 ## Less special occasions

You

For occasions that occur often, like going to the cinema or out to eat, how can I stop tics limiting what I do and where I go?

This month

Megan

Choose a venue. Every occasion has a range of venues, so try to choose a venue that makes tics less obvious – perhaps one that has some background noise and some privacy.

Dr Tara

Learn a skill. Pick a skill from the Tools section that is relevant to the venue and learn it. You will probably socialise often, so invest some time in a social skill (see Tools → Long term).

This week

Harry

Choose a time. Most venues have different clients at different times. Ticcing in a noisy, busy venue at rush hour is much less conspicuous than during a quiet afternoon. Some online venue reviews (e.g. Google) can tell you how busy a venue is at different times of the day.

Zak

Look for tolerant showings. Many venues have procedures or spaces for people who require privacy or make noise, such as parties

events

or cultural groups. Some cinemas have showings especially designed for more tolerant audiences, so ask about when these might be scheduled, or join a relevant social media group to be informed about them.

events

Jess

Plan ahead at an event. Whenever I'm going to a busy event where there are lots of people who don't know me, I get in touch with the venue or organiser in advance and describe the things that make me more comfortable. For me, these are my tics being acknowledged at the start of the event so people can understand and ignore them. I also check that there's a more private space that I can go to if my tics intensify. I might ask to sit near a door so I can get in and out easily if I need to. Being open and saying what you need can feel difficult at first, but the more you do it, the easier it becomes.

Tomorrow

Harry

Book a seat near the back. People will be less distracted by your tics. If you need space to tic, sit in the aisle or buy yourself a second seat, so there will be space beside you.

Today

events

Megan

Prepare yourself. Get your head into the right space and get your tics sorted with whatever tic management strategies you find work for you.

TOOLS

This section gives you the skills for living with Tourettes. Each part provides information or a skill you will need to face challenges and understand your condition well. So, what do you need to know?

What is Tourettes?

Here is the lowdown on what Tourettes actually is.

What are tics?

Tics are sudden, rapid, recurrent, non-rhythmic movements and noises. Although many people have the same sorts of tics (e.g. eye blinking, sniffing, throat clearing, head jerking), there are also tics that are specific to each person.

Tics are different to other motor conditions in that they change with time, can often be controlled for a period of time and are preceded by a sensation (which feels different for everyone but is similar to an itch), referred to as a 'premonitory urge' or 'tic signal'.

Dr Jolande

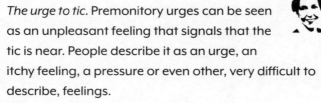

The urge to tic. Premonitory urges can be seen as an unpleasant feeling that signals that the tic is near. People describe it as an urge, an itchy feeling, a pressure or even other, very difficult to describe, feelings.

Duncan

Sense of frustration. Having tics feels a lot like being covered with mosquito bites. I didn't really have any extra energy until I was about six or seven, and then it came and moved in. It's like going through your day for eight hours being covered with poison ivy and not scratching.

Dr Jolande

Teach others how it feels. Would you like to show your friends or relatives why you HAVE to do your tics? Suggest that they do the following exercise:

Ask your friend or relative to open their eyes and stop blinking for as long as you tell them to. Ask them what they experience in their eyes when they stop blinking. Probably they will feel an urge to blink, an itchy feeling in their eyes or a pressure that builds up inside. Once you allow them to blink again, they will probably blink several times to get rid of this nasty feeling. Try it yourself!

🔧 Who has tics?

Most people's tics start between five and eight years of age. The first tics are usually eye blinking or head jerking. Then vocal tics such as sniffing or throat clearing may begin. Tics tend to change with time, with new tics emerging and old tics revisiting. A sudden new tic can be a surprise for people, particularly after a period of very few tics.

Prevalence

Between 0.5–1 per cent of children will have Tourettes. However, tics that occur for a shorter period of time than a year are very common in primary school-aged children. Studies show 4–22 per cent of school and preschool-aged children will have tics at one time or another. This shows the importance of teachers and other professionals who work with children understanding tics.

Adult onset

There are a small group of individuals who develop tics as adults. Very little research has been done on this group of people, but information shows that they are less likely to have co-existing difficulties than individuals with onset of tics in childhood. Adult-onset tics tend to wax and wane, occur mostly in males, be strong, and be both motor and vocal. For some people, tics start in childhood, then go away in the middle adult years, to then reappear in later years.

Tics can also occur following a brain injury or illness, so discuss a sudden onset of tics with your doctor.

For some people, the start of tics can happen after a traumatic event.

Demographics

In general, four times more males have tics than females. The reasons why more boys have tics than girls is not clear, but a similar ratio is seen in other neurodevelopmental conditions such as attention deficit hyperactivity disorder (ADHD), autism spectrum disorder (ASD) and specific learning disorders. We do not know if more males than females grow out of their tics, but scientists are looking at this.

Tics can be inherited from either parent. Life experience such as complications during childbirth and throat infections will also impact whether an individual expresses their 'tic genes'.

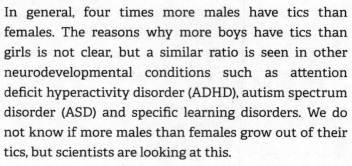

Getting a diagnosis of Tourettes

The diagnosis of Tourettes means that you have had motor tics and one or more vocal tics for longer than one year. People may have a suspicion that they have Tourettes, particularly if they have had tics for years, but do not get a formal diagnosis until they are a teenager or even an adult. You may have read about tics and diagnosed yourself, but many people also like to have a formal assessment, for clarity and to learn about treatment and strategies to help.

Find a health professional who can go through your medical history and hear about your tics. A checklist of tics is sometimes used to diagnose Tourettes, called the Yale Global Tic Severity Scale. It's good to find out that it's definitely tics and not something else that might be worrying you or your family. If your general doctor cannot help you, then ask them to refer you to a specialist who has training in diagnosing people with tic disorders.

what

Jess

It's worth getting a diagnosis even after years of having tics. I've had tics since I was a child, but I wasn't diagnosed until I was an adult. I knew I probably had Tourettes in my late teens but back then I didn't see what getting a formal diagnosis would add. I'm so glad that I was formally diagnosed because it meant I could finally understand something that had always been a part of my life.

If you have very few tics or they mainly occur in one particular situation, it can be helpful to record a video of your tics on a phone to show a health professional so that they understand and can see what you are talking about.

Duncan

It's Tourettes – what a revelation. I had almost finished high school. The newspaper column I was reading that day while eating was about Tourettes. It was the most pivotal moment of my life. My jaw dropped. The sandwich dropped. I read the article about three times and that voice that had always been sober in the back of my head was now doing handstands and cartwheels and going, 'That's me! That's me! That's me!'

what

When you are diagnosed, you will probably be asked about when and where the tics happen and what triggers them. It will also be helpful to let the health professional know about the pattern that your tics have taken, if the tics have been constant or if they have changed with time in type and frequency.

Jess

Waxing and waning. One of the trickiest aspects of life with Tourettes can be when tics suddenly change. Getting used to a new set of tics and working out strategies can be a tough process, but I've yet to find a tic that can't be managed with creative thinking, practical adjustments and openness.

Getting diagnosed accurately is a relief

The health professional who diagnoses you could be a neurologist (with an interest in brain conditions), a psychologist (who is interested in behaviour and thinking), a psychiatrist (with a special interest in psychiatric conditions such as ADHD) or perhaps a specialist nurse or occupational therapist. It's less the person's professional training that matters and more their knowledge of tics and Tourettes.

Duncan

Scientists can't decide what Tourettes is. Is it a psychological or neurological disorder? Well obviously it's both!

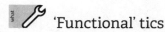 'Functional' tics

'Functional' tics are involuntary movements and sounds that typically result from an underlying difficult situational or psychological stress. Functional tics are fairly common but not well understood. Functional tics are more behavioural than Tourettes tics, which are more neurological. It is important to note that people with functional tics are not making the symptoms up. Functional tics often affect a person's major limbs but can also be smaller movements of the face and head and sounds. They can look somewhat similar to tics in Tourettes but follow a different pattern in terms of when they usually start, and they change less with time. People with tics as part of a tic disorder can also have functional tics. Functional tics often start very quickly and can be triggered by emotional or psychological stress. Functional tics can stop quite quickly and often occur with co-existing challenges such as anxiety. Functional tics are not preceded by a premonitory urge and are typically not suppressible. There is usually a less clear pattern to functional tics.

Functional tics can reduce when the person is distracted from the movements or increase if the person is being observed. Physiotherapy exercises have been shown to help with functional tics. Techniques for helping reduce organic tics (e.g. behavioural therapy and medication) do not often reduce functional tics, but treating an additional condition such as anxiety may be effective.

Tourettes plus other difficulties

Often it's not the tics that are a problem for people but other co-existing conditions. Most people (50–80 per cent) with Tourettes will have one of the following conditions and many will have two and possibly even three:

Attention deficit hyperactivity disorder

Attention deficit hyperactivity disorder (ADHD) is the most common co-occurring condition with Tourettes. It is described as a persistent pattern of inattention and/or hyperactivity-impulsivity that interferes with functioning or development, with difficulties noticed before 12 years of age. Throughout the world, the number of children with ADHD is thought to be about 3–10 per cent, with rates of about 4 per cent in adulthood. It is more common (2–4 times) in boys than girls. About 20–30 per cent of children with ADHD also have a tic disorder, and up to two-thirds of children with tic disorders will have ADHD.

The usual controls that most individuals can put on their thinking and behaviour are a challenge for those with ADHD. In the teenager years, a person with ADHD may make unnoticed errors in their work or be mistaken for day-dreaming or be very impulsive in their behaviour.

ADHD symptoms are usually seen before tics start, in the preschool or early school age years. Although it was previously thought that children grow out of ADHD symptoms as they mature into adults, it appears now that about half of all adults will continue to experience ongoing symptoms that can benefit from medication and/or cognitive behavioural therapy treatments.

If you have struggled with focus, impulsivity or being fidgety and are hyperactive in a way that impacts on your life, then discuss it with your doctor.

Obsessive compulsive disorder

Obsessive compulsive disorder (OCD) is a type of repetitive anxiety disorder where a person has trouble with frequent obsessions and/or compulsions that cause distress, take up time and get in the way of living their life.

It's helpful to know about the two aspects of OCD:

- *Obsessions* are recurrent and persistent thoughts, images or impulses that come into a person's mind without warning. Obsessions are often associated with feelings of fear, disgust, doubt or 'incompleteness'. Many people with Tourettes have a particular type of obsession, which tends to be a 'just right' feeling.

- *Compulsions* are repetitive, purposeful behaviours, often done in a certain way to neutralise or stop an obsessional thought or feeling. You can often see compulsions (e.g. touching or ordering objects), but sometimes they are just thoughts without an action.

Duncan

OCD and ADHD are different problems with inhibitions. It's basically dis-inhibition. What I mean by disinhibition is that the proper brakes/the proper sensors in the different areas of your brain don't work that well. They're disinhibited. With Tourettes obviously it's a motor brake that isn't working very well, so extra movements come out. With OCD it's a brake over your thoughts. They get stuck on like a broken record in people with OCD, and with ADHD it's the brakes over your attention, so you leap all over the place.

If compulsions or obsessions impact on your daily life, then seek help from your doctor; there are good treatments available.

Anxiety disorder

Anxiety is a natural feeling that gives the person an unpleasant feeling of apprehension. Most people with anxiety describe unpleasant physical symptoms such as racing heart rate, dry mouth and sweating, which occur due to adrenaline surging in the body as a result of worrying thoughts.

Anxiety is a response to a threat or perceived threat such as an exam or public speaking.

There are many different types of anxiety disorder that relate to the situation that causes you to feel anxious (e.g. intense fear of talking to people could be social anxiety). If you experience high levels of worry that stop you from doing the activities you would like to do, then speak with your doctor as anxiety disorders can be effectively treated with cognitive behavioural therapy and/or anti-anxiety medication.

Mike

Feel the fear and do it anyway. I think it's important to make it clear that everyone gets anxious in lots of situations. So having Tourettes is not a pass for avoiding life. Everyone has things they are worried about or are self-conscious about. The people who are engaged with life are the ones who turn up and deal with situations that challenge them. By doing so they also gain in confidence. And confidence solves a lot of problems.

Autism spectrum disorder

Autism spectrum disorder (ASD) is a developmental disorder that means that a person struggles to interact and communicate socially and has a strong tendency to enjoy repetitive behaviours and specific interests.

It's thought that 10–20 per cent of people with Tourettes may reach criteria for a diagnosis of ASD compared to 1 per cent of the general population. Mostly, ASD is diagnosed in childhood, but for some people, challenges with social interactions and restricted interests become most noticeable in teenage or adult years. There is no cure for ASD, so the most helpful thing is to learn about the condition, adapt your life and educate others.

Depression and suicidal thoughts

Depression is a condition in which a person feels 'miserable' and shows uncharacteristic behaviour. Any of us can feel like this from time to time, but if the symptoms persist for more than two weeks, then it is considered depression.

A person can have depressive feelings, behaviour and thoughts. Depressive feelings include feeling sad and fed up. Depressive behaviour includes tearfulness, becoming withdrawn, loss of interest in fun activities or hobbies and occasionally self-harm behaviour such as cutting oneself. Depressive beliefs are usually negative beliefs about oneself, other people and the future. Help is available for depression, so be brave and discuss it with your doctor.

Duncan

It's normal to feel overwhelmed and upset at times. I'd sit there in the corner of the bathroom and feel that I was completely and utterly alone. I was so lost, this was my mind. All sorts of emotions just scattered. I was a mess.

Suicidal thoughts are not uncommon in young people with Tourettes, although anyone can feel desperate at times. If you find yourself feeling very low and having thoughts about harming yourself, please speak with someone who can help. This person could be a family member, a friend or a health professional. There are very good ways to help people who worry about harming themselves, so do not keep these thoughts to yourself.

Anger and rage attacks

'Rage attacks' is the name given to a sudden angry response in a situation that does not really warrant it. This sort of response is quite common in people with Tourettes. It's often something that people feel bad about afterwards and wish never happened.

Rage attacks can impact on family, friends and relationships, so if you have these episodes it's worth discussing with a doctor. Although these symptoms tend to improve as people get older, if you feel that rage attacks impact your life, there are psychological and medical treatments available. The treatments are unlikely to take all of the symptoms away, but they can provide good strategies for managing common situations that provoke the attacks.

Headache

One of the most common medical conditions that people with Tourettes have is headache. More than 25 per cent of people (teenagers and adults) with Tourettes report an uncomfortable headache that might have other symptoms such as nausea (migraine) or not (tension-type headache). This compares with the general population in which about 3–5 per cent report chronic headache. The reason for frequent headache may relate to the chemical patterns in people's brain with Tourettes, or be due to tics involving repetitive head shaking, neck jerking and rapid shoulder movements.

There are medical and psychological treatments for persistent headache. If you find that the discomfort and pain impacts on your life, then discuss it with your doctor and ask for help.

Living with Tourettes
Tics as part of me

Accepting your tics

Accepting Tourettes as part of what makes you who you are is important because it lets you get on with making the best of who you are. Ask 'Who would you be if you woke up tomorrow and didn't have Tourettes?' Many people with Tourettes say that their tics are such an important part of who they are that they might even miss them if they disappeared.

Daniel

You are you, not your tics. Although tics are a part of who you are, so are hundreds of other qualities. Don't feel like you're defined by your disorder if you don't want to be.

People with Tourettes have less control of their bodies than other people, but they are not 'weird' or 'unwell'. Although you may not actually mean what you tic, it is a part of you. Tics are unique.

Duncan
Tics are better than fingerprints. We all have our distinctive barks.

Daniel
Tics are only embarrassing if you let them be. If you seem completely comfortable with your tics, then so will everyone else.

Advantages of tics

Tourettes can give people superpowers

People with Tourettes have advantages and strengths. One of these is the ability to deal with unpredictability. People with tics have had many years of managing quickly changing situations. One of the hallmarks of having tics is not knowing what is coming next and having to change to cope with a situation. Another superpower is the enormous self-control that people with tics have to use all the time when they want to control their tics. A few studies show this control can be used for other things. Having managed tics can make you resilient and flexible – different people gain different benefits from the experience.

Eliza

Having the actual tics didn't give me an advantage, but getting over it did.

Jess

See Tourettes the way you want to. I used to find it hard to talk about my tics but then I had a conversation with my friend Matthew. He described Tourettes as a 'crazy language-generating machine', and told me not doing something creative with it would be wasteful. This idea took root and was how I came to understand that my tics are my power, not my problem. Together we co-founded Touretteshero, an organisation that uses art and humour to increase understanding of Tourettes and support people living with the condition. We have a website and put on events. You can reach out at any time and find out how to get involved on our website, www.touretteshero.com (use the Safe Mode button on the website to hide anything rude).

Explaining your tics to other people

The world is full of people who don't know about tic disorders. Educate them.

Life is easier once you have a toolkit of solutions and the confidence to tell people about your tics

Officials

When you meet official people, it may be helpful to explain to them about your tics, so they can react in a helpful way. Tics are easily misunderstood, so make sure the official person understands the following:

- Tics are not meant to offend anyone.

- Tics are involuntary movements and sounds.

- You may need support in coping with tics in public.

- Show them the section For other people → Officials.

> **Daniel**
>
> *Try using metaphors for tics.* Tics can be hard to explain, but there's some great media out there to do the job for you. When I first started trying to explain tics I compared them to a cough, but looking back, it was a pretty bad metaphor.

Helpers

Telling your friends and family about tics is important so that they can help you and don't feel helpless or confused. If you're not keen to talk about tics again after this point, then let them know. It's also helpful to think about what to tell your girlfriend/boyfriend and when to tell them. Often partners have seen a lot of tics and they'll want to know how to help you. Arrange a quiet time to talk to other people about tics, and make sure you cover the following:

- Tics are involuntary movements and sounds that change often.

- Tics fluctuate.

- Unless you want to talk about tics, it's best to not comment on them.

- Tics are no one's fault.

- You may need help in advocating to gain support for your tics.

- Show the section For other people → Parents/Family members/Friends.

Sometimes friends and family may withhold information/not share secrets with you due to fears that you might say it in a vocal tic. This is something worth discussing with the person who holds the secret so that you can make a plan. A plan could be they tell you after they see the person.

Jess

Reach out to your friends for support.
Sometimes people can find it hard to know how to help when tics are tough. For me, other people's empathy makes a big difference. When my tics began affecting my mobility, a friend reassured me that it was a frightening situation and it was okay for me to be upset. This made me feel much more resilient.

Hinderers

Some people can be annoying (e.g. spreading gossip or misinformation, or teasing about your tics). If the person is annoyed by your tics, then discuss this with them and see what you or they can change about a situation to make it less annoying for you both. Let them know the following:

living

- Tics are involuntary movements and sounds.

- You'd prefer it if the person did not comment on your behaviour.

It is very common for people with tics to have to deal with comments and stares. Often, it's best to ignore this behaviour.

> **Daniel**
>
> *Rude people are just not worth it.* If someone's rude when asking about tics, they're probably just a rude person. I would calmly explain what tics are and make a note to avoid them in future.

Socialising

It's helpful to think about how much information you might want to share with someone at a party or social context about tics and what they'll be able to hear and understand over the loud music! Tell them the following:

- Tics are not meant to offend.

- Tics are involuntary movements and sounds.

- Tics are not contagious.

Avoiding stereotypes and misunderstanding

Some people are misinformed about Tourettes

There are many unfortunate stereotypes and common misunderstandings about Tourettes. This is partly thanks to the media, and misportrayal of the condition.

Obscene words or gestures (coprophenomena)
One of the biggest misunderstandings about Tourettes is that people think you must have swearing tics. This is

not true. Tourettes means you have had motor tics and one or more vocal tics for longer than one year.

Obscene words or gesture tics are called coprophe-nomena. Swearing tics, referred to as coprolalia, are about three times more common than rude gesture tics (called copropraxia). Coprophenomena tics are reasonably uncommon (experienced by about 10–20 per cent of people with Tourettes). Coprophenomena can start early or in the teenage years. Most people who have obscene tics find that they have started by 11 years. Coprophenomena tend to occur most often in people who have many other tics. Having one period of coprolalia or copropraxia early on does not mean that the person with tics would have it for life.

Mike

Using the label us up to you. The name 'Tourettes' is often equated only with uncontrolled vocalisation because there is a complete lack of understanding out there. I've said to a few people (with a bit of a laugh) that 'I never keep still' or similar if for some reason I've had to say something about the tics (which would only have been a few times over the years). I don't need a label, especially not at work.

Non-obscene socially inappropriate symptoms
Another stereotyped symptom in people with Tourettes is non-obscene socially inappropriate symptoms (NOSIS), which describes an urge to make insulting remarks, such as regarding a person's physical appearance (e.g. 'She is fat') or socially inappropriate behaviours (e.g. shouting 'bomb' on a plane). One study showed that about two out of three people with Tourettes (and many people in the general population) will have an urge to make these comments, but only about half of people with Tourettes NOSIS actually do the tics. For people with NOSIS, arguments with other people tend to be the most common negative consequence of the behaviour.

Dealing with coprophenomena and NOSIS is similar to dealing with other tics, except that you need to be even more assertive:

- Explain that tics are involuntary.

- You didn't mean what you said.

- Try to control the tics where possible.

- Keep yourself safe – don't go into situations where coprophenomena and NOSIS could be dangerous.

living

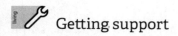

Getting support

Teaching mastery to others helps them and helps you both build a community

Family

Your family may be your primary support. Some of your family may have tics themselves (see Situations → Living with tics at home).

Duncan

Some problems are too big to fight alone.

There was something big. Bigger than I could explain that was scary, that I just felt helpless to do anything about.

Friends

Your friends might be another group of allies. Think which of your friends you want to talk to about having Tourettes (see For other people → Friends).

Jess

Humour can help. My friends ignore most of my tics but we laugh together at ones that are particularly funny or surprising. This feels very natural to me – humour has definitely helped me manage situations that otherwise might have felt tricky and upsetting.

Community

Many organisations may be able to help you and offer information. Organisations such as charities, health services and disability support departments can help you. Nearly all of these organisations will have a presence on the internet and social media – a simple search will give you an idea of what is available. Some people feel anxious about joining an organisation for people with tics, which is understandable. However, usually people in organisations are very knowledgeable and there is a rich environment for sharing information. Often people worry about stigma, but it seems that being open, honest and clear about the diagnosis is a good way to combat stigma.

Another way to gain community support might be to volunteer at an organisation (such as a youth group, football club or gymnastics group) where you can help people understand about what Tourettes is.

Finding support outside your friends, family and immediate network is a personal choice. Some people consider having Tourettes as a form of disability, whereas others have a different perspective and experience, due to tic severity, temperament, support, bullying and how other people respond.

Government

Governmental bodies have guidance on whether there is formal support for people with Tourettes. Look online or discuss with your doctor whether you might be entitled to the following support:

- Financial support if you cannot work due to Tourettes or associated conditions.

- Legal support if you are challenging an organisation that does not acknowledge your needs fully.

- Help from a carer to access public transport or with shopping.

School

Schools and colleges can offer you assistance, but you need to know who to ask, and what to ask for:

- There are many types of assistance (e.g. extra time, separate room, laptop typing, scribe, rest and exercise breaks, peer support, permission to record lectures). These differ between institutions and countries.

- The threshold for support will differ, so look on the relevant websites for information.

- Approach the person who deals with additional needs and present the information sheet that is given in the back of this book (see For other people → Teachers/lecturers).

- If you are not receiving the support you need, approach a senior member of staff at school such as the head teacher or the student union rep at university. Everyone will be happier if your tics do not distract others.

People might tell you that it's not fair to give some people extra time in exams, because it makes assisted people look better than they really are. Don't let opinions like this dissuade you from asking for the help you deserve that will allow you to show your abilities.

Suppressing tics

Suppressing tics is a personal choice. For some people, holding tics back during the day helps them to access work and education. For other people, tic control is very difficult. Others may choose not to control their tics as they feel that it impacts on concentration or even just 'being themselves'. It is important to know that no one can control all of their tics all of the time.

> **Mike**
>
> *Controlling your tics is up to you.* Sometimes when you're with your partner at home, and you're tired, it can be good to take a break for a short while from controlling the tics. But other

than that I don't want a 'pass' to tic at home. I prefer to require of myself to make an effort to control them. Most of the time I control tics, to some extent when alone, because I don't want to reinforce them. I don't put the same kind of effort in as when others are around, though.

For some people, the urge that goes before the tics can be annoying or uncomfortable. For many, controlling tics results in a reduction in this urge, but not for everyone. Even people who do not report a reduction in the urge say their tics can reduce with control, and the urge and tics can be much less bothersome. They realise that resisting the urge to tic will not result in any bad consequence. Psychologists call this 'expectancy disconfirmation', and it is useful to know that even if the urge to tic doesn't reduce when you control the tics, most people benefit from holding them in at times.

Myths about tic suppression
Nothing bad will happen if you suppress tics for a period of time. It doesn't hurt you.

There is an unhelpful myth around tics called the 'rebound effect'. The myth is that if someone controls their tics, then the tics could merely build up with time and 'explode' at a later point. The rebound effect has been disproven in laboratory experiments, in psychological treatments and in people's day-to-day life. There is no increase due to a build-up of tics. An example

living

is how at school many people (students and teachers) suppress the tics that they are not keen on their peers seeing or hearing. When they get home, they turn off the tic control and so they tic. Although they appear to have lots of tics, studies find that it is only half of the tics they had before they started controlling. Some people do tic more because people at home encourage tics by giving attention and allowances when the person has tics, so the tics are reinforced. This does not mean that the tics have been building up, but merely that the person adaptively puts the effort into where it best suits them to tic and not tic. Of course, when a person is tired or bored, the tics may come out then too, but they may also increase when someone is excited. There are no clear and consistent rules or reasons why tics go up and down.

The myth of the rebound effect

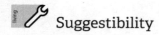

Suggestibility

Seeing other people who tic can cause you to tic too, regardless of whether they are actual tics or copied tics. Even thinking about tics can cause them to increase.

Seeing tics in another person may cause you to tic

Hey, I seem to have caught your tic!

Un-suggestibility of tics is also likely to be true – being with people who are calm can calm your tics.

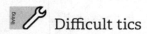

Difficult tics

Some tics are physically difficult or dangerous. Tics involving eye poking, teeth banging, hitting and touching other people can be particularly bothersome.

living

*Making a fuss about difficult tics
makes the situation worse*

Although difficult tics can feel overwhelming, there are effective and helpful ways to deal with them.

- Use all your force. The 'sledgehammer' solution of ERP works for all tics but you can only use it for short periods (see Tools → Treatments).

- Be creative. For other difficult tics it is about reducing the impact of each tic on your life.

- Protecting yourself can be helpful (such as, for sun-staring tics, wearing sunglasses or trying your best to not look at things).

- It may be helpful to sit away from another person.

- Put padding on your hands or wear a sports mouthguard if your tic is injuring (e.g. you are banging your teeth together).

- Avoid a majorly tic-inducing situation (e.g. screen-based games) or a particular trigger.

- Explain to other people that tics are real. An example of this might be if a stranger who sees you doing a body jerk tic on the train asks 'Are you just trying to get space here?' You could reply by saying 'It's a complex motor tic; I cannot help it.'

The repetition and overuse of a muscle to perform the tic can also cause you injury. Restraining yourself (e.g. putting hands in pockets) can help reduce the risk.

Some tics can be offensive to the person themselves or to other people, such as:

- sounds (grunts etc. might be taken as heckling)

- licking people/objects

- coprolalia – swearing

- copropraxia – rude gestures

- coprographia – writing obscene words

- non-obscene socially inappropriate symptoms (NOSIS).

For strategies to deal with difficult tics, see Tools → Obscene words or gestures (coprophenomena)/Non-obscene socially inappropriate symptoms.

Tic attacks

Tic attacks refer to an intense period of tics (organic or functional), which last from 15 minutes to several hours. Many people with tics report tic attacks, but little research has been carried out on the prevalence or nature of tic attacks.

Often the episodes are stressful and worrisome and can result in the person with the tic attack being assessed at emergency departments and undergoing unnecessary medical investigations due to concerns that the attack might be epilepsy or a brain infection.

The underlying cause behind tic attacks is often worries about tics that the individual may have. These concerns tend to grow as the person focuses their attention on the tics once the attack starts. The focus on tics then increases the worries about tics and leads the person to perform certain behaviours (referred to as 'safety behaviours') that they believe will stop the bad thing they are worrying about from happening. Unfortunately, this means that the person never finds out that the bad thing would not happen if they did not perform the safety behaviour and so they continue to do the safety behaviour, which can get in the way of everyday life. Two specialist health professionals, Dr Sally Robinson and Dr Tammy Hedderley, have put together the following model to illustrate how this association between tics and worries works.

living

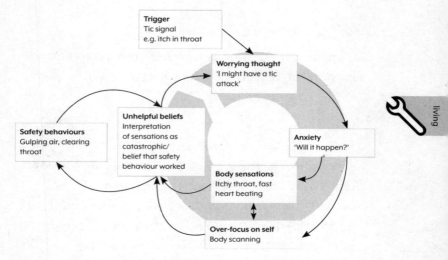

Adapted 'Psychological model of tic attacks'

Tic attacks are treatable. The first step is to understand what they are and what they are not. The second step is to map out the cycle above and manage anxious thoughts and associated safety behaviours to disrupt the cycle. You might like to get help from a psychologist for working on the tics, anxiety and safety behaviours.

Jess

Seek out support. When my tics intensified to a point where I was finding it hard to look after myself properly, I called my local adult social services team and they assessed my requirements. A support plan was put in place that gives me what I need to live a full and active life.

In society

An important question is whether your symptoms are *your* problem or a problem for society.

Jess

Learning about the social model of disability changed my life. This is a way of understanding disability which accepts that it's totally normal for bodies and minds to work in different ways, and for some people to have impairments and for others not to. Disability isn't caused by our bodies or minds, but by a failure to consider difference in how society is organised. I suddenly realised that I wasn't broken or faulty or the problem, but that the world needed to be set up in more inclusive and accessible ways in order to include me. Saying I'm disabled doesn't mean I'm less able; instead it acknowledges the barriers I face from environments, systems and attitudes that don't consider tics.

Mike

Talking about tics is up to you. Making allowances is a dance with society – you may have to modify your behaviour to fit in with society and perhaps people in society have to modify their attention to accept or ignore your tics. I don't tell my running friends about Tourettes while running because I don't want to be able to use it as an excuse for a bad performance. Otherwise, when things get tough in a race, it might be too easy to convince myself, 'Oh well, people will understand if I stop or slow down.'

I'm more than my tics

What can you do to avoid being thought of as just 'that person with Tourettes'?

When you have a condition like Tourettes which can be quite obvious to other people, it's helpful to make sure that you do not 'become Tourettes', that you are 'more than your tics'.

If a label has started to stick, make sure that you are getting on with your life:

- Try to be involved in situations and not avoid doing things or going places.

- Normalise situations quickly – ensure people see normal conversation and interaction, not just tics, when they meet you (people with tattoos on their face have a similar situation, that people just remember their tattoo).

- Give another person something positive to remember you for. Wow them with your charm or help them to hear your sense of humour. In this way, you choose your own label.

- Choose which tics you reduce, to control your image (e.g. 'No one cares if I blink, but they care if I lick them').

Stress management

Managing stress in life is a necessity for everyone but is particularly important if feeling stressed can result in more tics and less ability to cope with them. Everyone has different approaches, from controlled breathing to problem solving (see Tools → Problem solving).

Daniel

Manage stress. Stress can be a huge trigger for tics. Don't let that stress you out more. Take the time to calm yourself and deal with the situation, knowing that the tics will calm down again once you have.

Exercise

Mike

Use exercise to destress. During times of major stress, tics can be a bit more full-on. I find that exercise of some kind helps a lot. Firstly, because movement is always good, and secondly, because the exercise takes the edge off the stress, at least for a while.

Exercise is so important for helping you manage stress that it has its own section in this Survival Kit (see Tools → Exercise).

Relaxation

Relaxation alone is not an effective long-term treatment for tics. In the short term, relaxation might increase or decrease your tics, depending on the person and the relaxation activity. Some people believe that because tics increase as a result of stress, then relaxation exercises might reduce tics. Research shows that this is probably not the case in the long term. However, relaxation may help you to feel better and more prepared about approaching a task. It is important that you do the task, though – active strategies for tic control work best when practised.

Liz

Practise relaxation techniques you really like when calm and deliberately bring them to mind when stress appears. I have made an exercise called 'At ease with your tics: A guided relaxation' designed to help you to relax and calm the muscles around where you feel any individual tic originates and to observe and explore sensations and urges that you may feel just before a tic. You can return to the relaxation however often and whenever you want. The specially designed recording is just under 20 minutes long. You are asked to set your intention to be kind and compassionate with yourself and to set your intention to calm and relax the muscles in the area of your body you want to focus on. You are also asked to set your intention to observe and explore any sensations, urges and tics that come along with kindness and acceptance.

Problem solving

When you get into tricky situations, how do you deal with them?

Problems come in all shapes and sizes, and being able to deal with them is really important. The skill of problem solving needs practice, but the diagram below shows a good way of dealing with any kind of problem, whether it's large or small.

How to solve a problem

Liz

Problem solving. Be ingenious – think up possible solutions for each problem you have around tics and your range of coping solutions will grow.

Handling pressure

Pressure can make you stressed, and stress makes tics worse. There are ways to handle pressure so it doesn't cause stress:

- *Give yourself extra time:* Over-estimating task times makes it less stressful when things do go wrong (e.g. tics getting worse), and gives you time to make it 'great' rather than 'adequate'.

- *Acclimatise:* When you are used to pressure it doesn't stress you out as much. Start with self-pressure by setting yourself 'soft deadlines' to have things ready early. Then try to add extra features or quality.

- *Try to stay focused:* Many people report that their tics are much lower when they are focused, and people work much more effectively when focused 'in flow'.

- *Take regular breaks:* The few minutes you spend on a break quickly pays itself back in better efficiency and fewer errors.

- *Forget about tics:* Some days there is no time to focus much attention on tics, so just accept them for today.

Sleep

Sleep patterns can often be a challenge. The sorts of challenges people with Tourettes experience include sleepwalking, night waking and ticcing during sleep.

More than half of people with Tourettes experience poor sleep, and this increases if the person has additional co-existing difficulties.

Let people know the quirky things about tics

There are many strategies that you can do to improve your sleep:

- Do regular exercise and activities during the daytime and avoid too much strenuous exercise just before bedtime.

- Avoid food or drinks containing caffeine such as chocolate, coffee, tea or cola in the late afternoon or evening (within six hours of going to sleep).

- Avoid using a screen such as a tablet or computer screen for at least 90 minutes before you go to sleep as the screen light impacts on melatonin production, which is needed for helping you to get off to sleep.

- It is helpful to avoid having electronic equipment, particularly a phone or tablet, in the room once lights are out.

- Ensure your bedroom is dark, comfortable and cosy.

- Keep a bedtime routine and ensure bedtime and wake-up times are similar each day.

- Make a diary of what you do before bedtime, including the time you go to bed and then get off to sleep, to see if there are any unhelpful patterns.

- If you sleepwalk, make sure that exit doors are safely locked and that people you live with are aware of the behaviour so that they are not surprised if they meet you unexpectedly.

If you do not find that these strategies improve your sleep, then book a time to see your doctor and request a referral to see a sleep specialist. If the cause of sleep difficulties relates to anxiety, then it's worth getting help for that too.

Self-medicating

Self-medicating is a term for when people use substances to stop feeling a certain way or doing a certain thing. Some of the substances can be bought over the counter, such as homeopathic treatments like Bach Rescue Remedy. Other substances may be alcohol or non-prescription drugs such as smoking cannabis, which may be illegal. In fact, taking cocaine may actually increase tics. We recommend that you discuss any substances you take with your doctor to make sure that they are safe for you. Non-prescription drugs and alcohol may interact with medications prescribed by your doctor.

Self-esteem

Looking after your body can help tics and build confidence. It may also result in higher levels of energy and stamina, which might be helpful in managing tics, which can be tiring, both physically and mentally.

> **Mike**
>
> *Being active helps massively.* The exercise takes the edge off a lot of tics and also helps me feel more relaxed. It also makes me feel good about myself physically, which is important because the sensations of Tourettes makes me aware of my body a lot of the time.

Diet

Eat a well-balanced diet with regular meals and plenty of fruit and vegetables. There is no scientific evidence that any food in particular causes or increases tics. The only finding from studies is that consuming caffeine may increase tics for people with Tourettes.

Positive attitude

Having a positive attitude is important. If you smile, people will forgive most things. If you're struggling in a situation, focus on what you *can* do. If you would like people to ignore the tic, then focus on making that happen and don't get distracted.

If you smile, people will forgive most things

Exercise

> You used to hate ticcing, but you're now so strong that you don't seem to care about the tics.

Looking after your body can build confidence, which helps you deal with tics because you're not focused on them

Daniel

Staying in shape boosts confidence massively, making it easier to deal with other problems in your life, including tics.

living

Mike

After extreme exercise, tics can sometimes be worse for a while (or, more likely, the mental energy to manage them is more limited). But overall, being physically active definitely takes the edge off tics as you go about your life.

Many people with tics say that exercise reduces the tics. We don't know specifically which exercise helps, how much exercise helps, or how often. Experiment with what works best for you.

Mike

Explosive exercise helps a lot – boxing, for example (can be with a bag, or in an exercise class for those who don't want to train for actual boxing).

Rupert

The onset of a tic can disrupt the element of exercise that you are doing at the time, such as a vocal tic, which leaves you short of breath, or a motor tic, which makes you stop what you were doing.

If tics interrupt your performance, make sure that the coaches or adjudicators in the sport are aware of the diagnosis and how it impacts on you and your play.

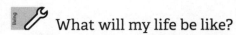 ## What will my life be like?

The future is an important question for many young people with tics. Research from Denmark which tracked children with tics for six years from when they were 12 years old showed that about 80 per cent grew out of most of their tics by the time they were 18 years old.

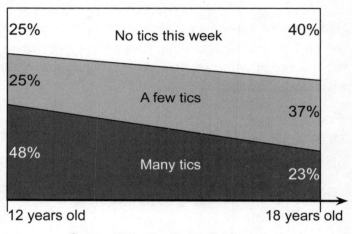

25%   No tics this week   40%

25%

A few tics

37%

48%

Many tics

23%

12 years old   18 years old

The number of tics in the last week, for people with Tourettes

Daniel
Don't waste time waiting to outgrow tics; it might never happen, and you have to be ready to accept that.

Having severe tics in childhood appears to be a strong predictor of having severe tics in adulthood.

Success in work is not related to having tics. There are many successful people with Tourettes in all sorts of professions.

Liz

Coping with the fact there is no cure. After you've realised Tourettes isn't expected to get worse over your adult lifetime, there's lots of management techniques to try!

 ## Other people with Tourettes/tics

Many people with tics don't know anyone else with Tourettes. There are reasons for and against meeting other people with tics.

Hanging out with other people who have Tourettes
Pros:

- *Not feeling alone:* Many people with tics feel less alone with their condition when they spend time with other people who have Tourettes. A shared experience and understanding is useful.

Liz

Go to a support group, even a few times. It's such a relief to be yourself and see all the tics that you thought only you had are so similar in other people. You're not alone!

Jess

Find some friends with tics. Meeting other people with Tourettes was an important part of accepting my own tics. I realised that I would never expect anyone else to hold their tics in or be embarrassed by them, so I didn't need to expect that of myself. Meeting other people with Tourettes for the first time can be nerve-racking but it can also be life-changing. I've made incredible friends and feel part of a vibrant and accepting community.

Duncan

Find similar folk. The first person I ever met with Tourettes... We had that same disinhibited energy, you know, our thoughts jumping around. In those first four seconds we had not only decided we loved each other, but we covered about 86 topics.

- *Share coping strategies:* People can share practical tips on how to cope with everyday life that have worked well for them.

- *Inspiration:* Seeing other people with Tourettes who have succeeded can help you understand that tics need not limit your life. Not convinced? This book is peppered with advice from successful people with Tourettes.

Cons:

- *Shyness:* Some people don't talk because they don't know what to say (or what not to say). There may be people in your own family with tics and speaking with them could be easier than with a stranger. Or not.

living

- *Disassociation:* Some people who have mild Tourettes don't feel it is a major part of who they are. People with red hair don't necessarily talk to each other, and people with mild tics might feel the same way.

Mike

Friends with tics is not for everyone. Personally I wouldn't want to hang around with anyone, or meet with anyone, because they have tics. That is because it's not a big part of my identity, and I'm happy with that. I also wouldn't avoid someone who had tics – the tics aren't a determining factor either way for whether I spend time with someone. Of course if someone needs a support group, that would be different.

- *Embarrassment:* Some people prefer not to spend time with other people who have tics, or even talk about it. This may come from negative feelings about their tics. Some people feel horrified at the idea of being part of a group of people all ticcing; other people feel liberated.

- *Tic suggestibility:* Sometimes another person's tic can make you tic like them – both in timing and type. Other people with tics could worry about catching new tics.

Telling people who are unaware that they have Tourettes

Once you know what tics are, you may see them often. Should you tell the person with the tics? There is no clear answer, so think about these possibilities:

Pros:

- They may not know what their movements or sounds are, so they could be worried.

- You could be the first person to share expertise on tics with the individual, which could change their life or at least their understanding of tics.

Cons:

- It may be that the person already knows but doesn't feel like talking about it. Sounding out whether they would want to know would be helpful before diving in with a full-fledged discussion.

- It could be embarrassing for the other person if they don't want to believe they have Tourettes or prefer to believe that nobody else notices.

Mike

Why tell someone if they have tics? Leave them to it unless they obviously need or seek help or support.

 ## Treatments

Although there is no cure for tics, there are treatments that can help people to live with the symptoms and reduce tics.

 ## Immediate help

Sometimes you need immediate help with the tics you are having today.

Tic triggers

Get to know the triggers that seem to make your tics happen more. Research shows that being tired, excited, stressed or physically unwell can exacerbate tics. You will likely have your own triggers. Monitor the pattern of your tics and ask a close friend or family member for their observations. Examples of triggers might be having to speak publicly at work, sitting on busy public transport or playing a game.

Once you have a sense of your current tic triggers, change elements of your everyday routine to minimise the impact of the tics. For tics triggered by playing on your computer, try to play the computer for limited periods and not before you go somewhere important or demanding. Instead use relaxation exercises at these times and plan some downtime or use a behavioural therapy that works for you. Be careful not to change your routine so much that you start to avoid situations or activities.

> **Mike**
>
> *Avoid uncomfortable clothes.* Some clothes can create tics (the fabric, the way they rest, type of collar, etc.). It sounds obvious, but don't wear those clothes! Do yourself a favour and wear the clothes that make you feel comfortable.

Pacing

Boom and bust patterns: Loading yourself up with too many demands or tasks can be unhelpful, especially if it continues for several weeks so you get burnt out and unable to deal with it. This pattern is called a 'boom and bust' cycle in which you do too many things (i.e. 'boom') which results in being unable to cope (i.e. 'bust'). Here's what you can do:

- Pace yourself and know your limits. Spread out your time and effort. Don't agree to take on too many tasks at once. It's okay to say, 'No thanks, I'm not able to do that now.'

- In the short term, allow yourself to stop an activity and take a walk, get a drink, chat with a friend or gaze into the distance for a few minutes.

Breathing and mindfulness

Breathing slowly when you're in a crisis can give you time to think about and understand what is happening. It won't change the problem but it may change how you see it and how you respond to it. So take a deep breath if something unexpected happens. There is growing evidence for mindfulness exercises that can provide a sense of calm and containment.

Positive mindset

Re-evaluating negative or difficult thoughts (which psychologists call 'cognitive restructuring') can be very helpful. It may be that you have gotten into a habit of feeling that nothing is possible and having tics is ruining your life. Evaluating these self-doubting thoughts could be very helpful in terms of what is realistic and what is not. It could be useful to do this with a therapist or someone who cares about you and can give another point of view.

Liz
Find some heroes who inspire you, from Tourettes folk you admire and celebrities with Tourettes!

Disguise

Some people disguise their tics, such as wearing loose clothing that doesn't show stomach tics. Disguise can help get you through a tricky situation, but it probably won't reduce the tics in the long term.

Distract

Chewing gum or sucking on sweets can distract from the need to tic. Letting energy out in other ways rather than ticcing can be helpful. There is some evidence that having a movement near your body such as a vibrating watch can distract from tics.

Mike
Just jigging your legs can be helpful to release some energy and avoid ticcing.

 ## Long term

There are skills that you can learn to reduce tics in the future.

Behavioural therapy

Behavioural therapy reduces tics by teaching new patterns of action. There are two effective types of behavioural therapy – 'habit reversal training' and 'exposure and response prevention'.

Dr Jolande
In several guidelines, behavioural therapy is described as the first step in treating people with tic disorders.

Dr Jolande

I'm so glad that more and more young people can profit from behavioural therapy these days! That means less medication, less side effects and happier families.

If you are interested in behavioural therapy, then discuss it with your specialist. Many charities have a list of therapists who have training and experience in offering the treatment, so you could contact them too.

HABIT REVERSAL TRAINING

Habit reversal training uses the person with tics' awareness of when a tic is coming to allow them to intervene with a competing response (a 'tic blocker') to stop tics from occurring.

The treatment focuses on controlling one tic at a time, in four steps:

1. The therapist and person select the most annoying tic to work on.

2. A detailed description of the tic is made. The therapist breaks down the tic to understand where the urge occurs, then what each element of the tic is.

3. Once the form of the tic is clear, the therapist and person work together to devise the competing response that the person uses after they feel the urge to tic and before they tic.

4. The person then practises using the 'tic blocker' as much as they can in places that they want to have fewer tics. It might take a little time to get the tic blocker to work well, but when it does, it's a great strategy.

The person selects the next most annoying tic and the process is repeated. Typically, treatment lasts for 8–12 sessions but this will depend on how many tics you have and how long it takes to get a result.

Dr Jolande

Get down with the detail. In 'habit reversal treatment', the youngster and I analyse the tic detail by detail. It's quite interesting how we can sometimes talk for about 15 minutes about a tic that lasts for only a second! Often we discover new things about the tic, for example that your nose moves too when you blink your eyes, or that it's always the left eye that closes first, before closing the right eye. If you can identify the first part of the tic and stop it, then you can stop the whole tic!

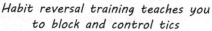

Habit reversal training teaches you to block and control tics

A well-validated programme of habit reversal training for adults and children with tics is called 'Comprehensive Behavioural Intervention for Tics' (CBIT). CBIT has been delivered with groups in many ways, using telemedicine, on a website and by professionals other than psychologists. A large study of CBIT was carried out in the United States. Half of the adults and two-thirds of the children responded well to the treatment.

They typically experienced a 40–50 per cent reduction in tics and improvements in daily activities and mood.

EXPOSURE AND RESPONSE PREVENTION

In exposure and response prevention (ERP), the point of the intervention is to help the person get used to feeling the 'tic signal' that occurs before they tic, and then not do the tic. This treatment has two main steps:

1. *Response prevention:* In the beginning, the person practises suppressing their tics for as long as possible using any strategy they can.

2. *Exposure and response prevention:* Once the person is confident with controlling tics for a few minutes, the exposure element of ERP starts. The person is encouraged to feel the urge to tic as strongly as possible without ticcing. Then the time is increased. The person sits with the urge until it reduces or stops bothering them. Resisting the urge is difficult but gives you a tool to control tics.

The patient learns to control all of their tics at once. Frequent practice of ERP is important. Treatment is usually given in 8–12 appointments.

Dr Jolande

A great brain workout. 'Exposure and response prevention' in tic disorders is one of my favourite treatments. In this therapy, I coach youngsters to withhold all their tics as long as possible.

I love seeing these proud faces when they can control their tics for longer and longer. In almost everyone I see an improvement in withholding times during the session. When a patient becomes too good, it's my job to make it harder. I try to provoke the urge to tic and must be quite creative to do so!

ERP studies show it is a very promising treatment. One study followed adults and children one year after treatment and showed that their tics had reduced by 50–60 per cent. ERP was similarly effective to medication and was far more popular amongst participants. ERP is available over telemedicine and is being trialled for delivery online and in groups.

Either habit reversal training or exposure and response prevention is usually combined with learning about tics (psychoeducation), identification of triggers for tics, relaxation techniques and finding ways for your family or friends to help you work through the programme.

Cognitive behavioural therapy
A second wave of treatments, such as cognitive behavioural therapy, focuses on changing negative thoughts and feelings associated with tics, to aid coping. The treatments also feature a behavioural strategy to manage the tics.

'Third wave' treatments
There are other forms of behavioural treatment that are starting to be studied more, such as acceptance

and commitment therapy. These are often referred to as the 'third wave' treatments. They focus on sitting with and accepting the urge that precedes tics. The difference between 'third wave' treatments and ERP is the perspective that the person is invited to take. The focus is on accepting the urge to tic, not fighting or controlling it.

Medication

There is good evidence that taking medication which changes the chemicals (referred to as neurotransmitters) in your brain can reduce tics. Many psychotropic medications that are used to treat other conditions are also safe and effective for tics. Your doctor can advise you on which psychotropic medication will suit you. For treating psychosis (antipsychotics), the brand names are Aripiprazole and Risperidone, for blood pressure (antihypertensives), the brand names are Guanfacine and Clonidine. Taking medication is far less work than behavioural therapy, but it's likely that tics increase when medication is stopped. As with all medication, some people will suffer side effects, which could include weight gain, difficulties with sleep, dizziness and flattened mood.

There is some evidence for taking cannabinoids in reducing tics. Although more research is needed, with a controlled and monitored dose some individuals with tics find a reduction in their symptoms. It is not recommended that you experiment with recreational drugs yourself, but instead discuss with your specialist about research in the area.

Dr Jolande

Meds are an option but beware. In the early days, a lot of medication was prescribed for both children and adults with these complaints. Although they can have a positive effect on tics, many patients suffer quite severe side effects like weight gain and sleepiness.

 Brain treatments

For people with very bothersome or life-threatening tics, invasive interventions such as deep brain stimulation (DBS) can be helpful. DBS is when an electrode is placed in the brain of the person who has tics, within the part of the brain that is believed to underlie the tics (cortical thalamic subcortical circuitry). The electrode, which is attached via wires to a small box, vibrates within the person's brain, which results, for many, in a reduction of tics. Anyone who is considering DBS will have first considered and tried several forms of medication and behavioural therapy. In most countries DBS is only offered to adults, because many young people grow out of most of their tics.

Transcranial magnetic stimulation (TMS) is another direct brain treatment. In TMS, a magnet is used to stimulate the brain from outside, which is thought to change brain activation and result in fewer tics. A few studies have found that stimulating the part of the brain that controls movement is the most effective.

Early research suggests that younger individuals who also have ADHD benefit the most.

What doesn't work

Some interventions have been researched and shown not to help reduce tics.

Counting tics

Some treatments in the past have asked people to count their tics for a certain period of time each day. The idea with this was to build up an awareness of the tics in order for the person to work on them. Studies have shown that counting tics does not help to reduce them.

Massed practice

In the past, there was an idea that if you did a tic again and again, it would tire out the muscle that was doing the tic (called 'massed practice'), and the tic would reduce. We now know that tics come from the brain and are expressed in the body, so having a tired body is no help at all in reducing tics, and repeated practice actually strengthens the brain pattern of tics.

Punishment

Punishing yourself to stop tics is unlikely to help tics. Punishment is more likely to make you feel negative about yourself and your tics, which could impact your whole life, and not just your tics.

Duncan

Don't beat yourself up about it. I'd get so angry I'd think 'I'll just show it', so I'd tic and I'd hit myself. And I'd say, 'See, you freak, that's what happens when you do bizarre, weird dumb stuff like that, you know you get hit. It's not fun; it hurts. So cut it out. Don't do it any more. Quit it.' Then I'd tic again and say, 'That's stupid, you're not going to learn that you don't do this stuff', and I'd tic again and I'd hit myself again. I'd be ticcing more and more and more. I'd be hitting myself more and more, and eventually I'd just give up.

Staying at home

Dropping out of life is not really an option for managing tics. It may be necessary to take a rest or a break, or to pause and plan your approach if the situation is difficult. If you start to reduce the activities you do, patterns of behaviour build up very quickly and you might start to do fewer and fewer things and then your life can become very small. Avoid avoidance.

What has no evidence but people try anyway

Tics come and go of their own accord, so it's difficult to know if a treatment is really working. Well-designed research shows what works and what doesn't. To date, none of the items in the following list have been tested, so there is no scientifically proven evidence yet that they reduce or cure tics. It makes sense to be sceptical about advice from non-scientific resources.

Many people with tics make changes to their lives or try treatments in the hope that these might result in fewer tics. Some changes that haven't been proven are:

- eating organic food
- regular massage
- applying cranial osteopathy
- use of reflexology
- application of dental orthotics (mouth braces).

Ending – when to stop reading

You have learned a toolbox of strategies. Now choose what to do with this book:

1. *Give me away.* You've learned all you need and can share the book with someone else who knows far less than you.

2. *Keep me for a rainy day.* Having a toolkit could be helpful for you or someone you care about. You don't need to read this book cover to cover; this book is flexible – you can pick it up and read a section whenever you need to.

3. *Use me as a resource.* This is just the beginning of your education and involvement in Tourettes. Learn new tools as you need them. Show and lend me to other people.

ACKNOWLEDGEMENTS

There are many great people to acknowledge.

The first thanks goes to the young people who joined our focus group at Great Ormond Street Hospital Tourette Syndrome Clinic – Charlie Scott Vickers, Ashleigh Irvine and Lily Bradley Dickson. They sensibly advised us that young people were not that keen on struggling through traditional books, and suggested that we think of something different.

Huge thanks also to the other young adults with Tourettes – Charlotte Rushton and Charlie Langley – for their extremely valuable comments on the book. Thoughtful and constructive suggestions around layout were offered by Chloe Taylor and Dr Bethan Davies.

The advice in this book came from Dr Tara's many years of working with amazing and inspiring people who have tics.

Most of all we would like to thank our support crew (Daniel, Duncan, Eliza, Jess, Liz, Mike, Rupert and

Dr Jolande) who contributed the great advice you have seen throughout this book.

This book is dedicated to Dr Dunc, and all the professionals working with people who have Tourettes.

FOR OTHER PEOPLE

This section is for you to show to other people. These handouts can be downloaded from www.jkp.com/voucher using the code TAEFEKA

 **Parents**

[Give this to your mother and/or father]

If you are reading this section then you are a parent of a young person with tics. It will really help them cope with tics if you can understand tics.

Here's what you need to do:

- **Be strong.** Although you may feel sorry, guilty or overwhelmed by your young person's tics at times, do your best not to show or discuss these emotions with your young person.

- **Don't comment on tics.** In general, it's a good idea to not comment on your young person's tics unless they want to speak about them and how they affect their life.

- **Find strategies.** Understand if any tics cause your young person embarrassment, discomfort or pain, and help them to work out practical strategies to deal with the situations.

- **Help explain.** It might be very helpful if you can explain about your young person's tics to other family members so that they are sensitive and silently supportive around your young person. Ask your young person how they would like you to explain to family members and close friends about the tics.

- **Bully-proof them.** Most young people with Tourettes do not get bullied. Help your young person to be confident with their tics to minimise the likelihood of being a target of bullying.

- **Advocate for your young person.** Although they may have grown in confidence, it's likely that your young person will still need you to advocate for them every so often. This might be in relation to education, work environments, social interactions or within the family.

- **Get information.** There are many helpful and well-informed websites available about tic disorders. Look up your national charity and specialist clinics that often have sensible material.

- **Understand tics.** Know that tics fluctuate and change with time. Most young people grow out of many of their tics, but some continue to have a few tics in adulthood.

- **Choose the right treatment.** Your young person might need your help in seeking and accessing evidence-based treatment for tics.

- **Lift your head up and be proud of your son or daughter.** Living with tics is not easy.

parent

Family members

[Give this to your brother and/or sister]

One of your family members has Tourettes. Life is going to be easier for you and them if you do a few simple things to help them:

- **Learn about Tourettes.** Tics are involuntary, change with time and will come and go. Although they can be controlled sometimes, it's really hard work to control them, and it's really tiring.

- **Be patient with your brother or sister's tics.** It's not their fault that they tic, and they certainly don't do it to annoy you.

- **Don't comment on tics** unless they ask you about them.

- **Laugh with them, not at them.** Humour around tics is fine, as long as the person with tics sets the tone and is the first one to laugh.

- **Tell your friends not to comment on tics** when they come around to visit.

- **Look out for your sibling** at school, in the neighbourhood or within the family.

- **Be understanding.** Understand that your brother or sister might feel upset about having tics (or other things) sometimes, and try to reassure and help them with these feelings if they ask you to do so. Be kind and not snarky if the tics are loud or annoying. They could consider moving to another room, or you could choose to be somewhere else.

- **Invite them to do things.** Focused activities such as drumming and running can help with tics, so invite them to do something like this if you see that their tics are getting to them.

- **Tell them that you care for them** and don't care about the tics.

- **Read the rest of this book.**

Friends

[Give this to your friend when you both are ready]

One of your friends has got Tourettes. It's time to be the kind of friend you would like someone to be to you if you had a challenge. Having Tourettes means your friend has tics – involuntary movements and sounds that they can control for only a short time, sometimes with huge effort. Tourettes is different to other conditions because everyone can see the tics, even if they don't understand them or how to respond to them.

- **Tics don't mean there is anything else wrong with your friend that you should worry about.** Don't make a big deal out of the tics.

- **Helping explain tics to other people when your friend is too shy, angry or unable to would be great.** Don't be afraid to jump in and explain about the tics if your friend is unable to.

- **Tics change with time and fluctuate day by day.** Be patient with your friend's tics and expect them to be different over time.

- **Your friend is likely to cope well.** Don't let other people's reaction affect you or them.

- **Tics are not contagious.** You don't need to worry about catching tics.

- **It's okay to laugh at your friend's tics if they are laughing too,** but otherwise please don't comment.

- **Sometimes your friend might feel a bit down about the tics.** Your reassurance about how things will be okay can be really helpful. Tics are no one's fault.

- **Having tics shouldn't impact the way your friend handles life,** but stress might make their tics more frequent. It could be positive stress (winning a tennis game) or negative stress (preparation for exams). Don't be alarmed if your friend tics more in these sorts of situations.

- **Let your family know about your friend's tics** if your friend is coming over to visit. Explain to your family how it's best to ignore the movements and sounds unless your friend wants to talk about it.

friend

Girlfriends/boyfriends

[Give this to your girlfriend/boyfriend when you are both ready]

 The person who gave you this has tics or Tourettes. Tics are involuntary movements and sounds, which you have probably noticed already. Tics can be most frequent when a person is nervous, about to go to sleep or tired. Everyone's tics are different and they cope with them differently. Your support and understanding is going to be important in helping them to live with their tics, no matter how mild or severe the symptoms are.

Here are some things to know:

- **Most people get used to tics** and barely notice them after a while.

- **Tics can be humorous, but don't laugh at them** unless you are invited to do so.

- **It's likely that a person will have tics on and off.** The tics may change with time and it's unlikely that the person will know why. Sometimes tics develop from a behaviour such as sniffing as part of a cold, but often they just appear.

- **Tics can happen any time,** including intimate times, but rarely get in the way.

- **Gentle ignoring of the tics can help.** If your partner wants to talk about the tics, they'll let you know. This may only be once or it could be often. Ask them.

- **Tics can be controlled for short periods**, but this requires a lot of effort and prompting to do so will not be helpful.

- **Having tics is tiring**, but in general having Tourettes should not impact on any of the activities your partner is able to do, unless the tics are severe.

- **It may be helpful for you to attend an appointment** with a health professional to learn about tics and Tourettes.

Teachers/lecturers

[Give this to your teacher/lecturer before the start of the academic year]

If you are reading this section, then you are a teacher or lecturer of a student with tics. Tics are involuntary movements and sounds. The person does not choose to do tics, and although they may be able to control them for brief periods, they will not be able to do so for long periods of time.

It may be that you have never even noticed your student's tics, but now that you know what tics are, it might be obvious. Tics are common but don't always impact on the individual's life. It will really help your student if you can understand about tics.

Here's what you can do:

- **Get information.** There are many helpful and well-informed websites available about tic disorders. Look up the national charity for the condition (e.g. Tourettes Action in the UK) or clinics in specialist hospitals (e.g. Great Ormond Street Hospital in London, UK) as they often have sensible material available. Know that tics fluctuate and change with time.

- **Transitions are difficult for all young people.** It would be most helpful if you can offer support from the start of your student's journey at school/college/university.

- **It's a good idea to not comment on the student's tics** unless they want to speak about them and how they affect their life.

- **The student should be entitled to additional support** and access arrangements/accommodations within the classroom and for exams. Discuss these inputs with the student to see what works for them and then facilitate the appropriate applications. It may be helpful to liaise with the school's Special Educational Needs Coordinator who can help obtain a supporting report from a health professional.

- **Understand if tics cause them embarrassment, discomfort or pain,** and help them to work out practical strategies to deal with the situations.

- **It might be very helpful if you can explain about the student's tics** to other staff members so that they are sensitive and silently supportive. Ask the student how they would like you to explain.

- **Let your student know that you are aware of their difficulties** but see their potential and believe in them.

- **The student should be able to remain in the classroom for most of their lessons.** It will be helpful to think about where they sit to help manage the tics, and this should be discussed with them.

- **It can be helpful for the person to leave the room in quiet situations such as tutorials,** but the

teacher

student should be encouraged to attend as much of the school day or course as possible. Again, this should be discussed with the student, and may depend on the severity of the tics at a particular time.

- **Charities have developed helpful material** such as the Tourettes Action Passport by Tourettes Action in the UK, which can be found on their website and is available for all students with Tourettes.

- **Advocate for your student** and expect of them what you expect from your other students.

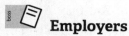 ## Employers

[Give this to your employer when you are ready]

You have an employee with tics and possibly Tourettes.
 Tics are involuntary movements and sounds. The person does not choose to do tics, and although they may be able to control them for brief periods, they will not be able to do so for long periods of time.

Tics are common but don't always impact on the individual's life. It will really help your employee if you can understand about tics and make the appropriate adjustments needed for them to work well for you.

Here's what you need to do:

- **Expect of the person** the same quality of work that you expect from your other employees.

- **In general, it's a good idea to not comment on the individual's tics unless they want to speak about them.** Make a specific time to discuss how tics might impact on the employee, their colleagues and their job. Know that tics fluctuate and change with time.

- **New jobs are difficult for many young people.** It would be most helpful if you can offer support from the start of employment.

- **The employee will be entitled to reasonable adjustments to facilitate their work environment.** Discuss these inputs with the employee and see what works for them. You may need to see a supporting letter or report from a relevant health professional, which the employee will be able to provide.

- **Understand if tics cause the employee discomfort or pain,** and help them to work out practical strategies to deal with the situations.

- **It would be very helpful if you can explain about the employee's tics** to other colleagues so that they are sensitive and silently supportive. Ask the employee if they would like you to explain or perhaps have your support when they do so themselves.

- **Provide the employee with contact details** so that they can communicate with you outside of working hours in the event that they need to let you know about a change in their symptoms, which can happen quickly.

- **If possible and appropriate, allow the employee to sometimes work from home** and check in with you at the end of the day on days when tics are severe or particularly bothersome.

- **Let your employee know that you are aware of their difficulties** but see their potential and believe in them.

- **Get further information.** There are many helpful and well-informed websites available about tic disorders. Look up your national charity and specialist clinics that often have sensible material.

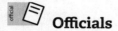 **Officials**

[Give this to an official on public transport/librarian/ cinema/bouncer at a club, etc.]

The person who gave you this has Tourettes. Tourettes is a brain condition in which the person has tics. Tics are involuntary movements and sounds.

The person does not choose to do tics.

Here's what you can do:

- **Believe the person.** The person may have some small movements and sounds that they cannot fully control. .

- **Allow them to go about their business.** Tics are not meant to offend anyone. The person won't cause trouble.

- **Ask if there is anything that you can do to help them.** It is hard to cope with tics in public.

- **Make 'reasonable adjustments'.** Consider simple things like letting them skip the queue line.

- **Be kind.** Imagine that this was a member of your family.

- **Do not accuse** the person of doing the tics on purpose.